ESSENTIAL FRENCH VERBS
Your Guide

Val Levick

Glenise Radford

Alasdair McKeane

HOW TO USE THIS BOOK

The verbs included in this book are those which students will meet and need to know, or at least recognise.

The book is divided into five sections:

Section 1 (pages 1-11) explains **how to use French verbs**.

Section 2 (pages 12-28) deals with **regular verbs** and common "nearly regular" verbs which have one example printed out in full, followed by a list of those common verbs which follow the same pattern.
There is also information about reflexive verbs.

Section 3 (pages 29-64) is an alphabetical list of common **irregular verbs** with the most common forms given in full.

Section 4 (pages 65-70) is a **French-English index** of all the verbs included, together with the number of the page where you will find them.

Section 5 (pages 71-76) is an **English-French index** of all the verbs included, together with the number of the page where you will find them.

Section 6 (page 77) is a **Grammar index**.

Inside the back cover: How to find the verb in this book

Throughout we have marked verbs which take **être** in the perfect and pluperfect tenses with an *.

SECTION 1 - HOW TO USE FRENCH VERBS

TENSES AND PARTS OF FRENCH VERBS

The tenses and parts of French verbs which are given in this book are those which will be of most use to students. It is not a complete list of all the tenses.

The **Infinitive** is the "name" of the verb and it is the form in which it will be found in a list of words or a dictionary:

    travailler - *to work*   **finir** - *to finish*   **répondre** - *to answer*

The **Present Tense** is used for:
* events which are taking place at this moment in time
* events which take place regularly
* events in the near future which are certain
* events which started in the past but are still continuing
  J'habite Malvern depuis deux ans *I have been living in Malvern for two years*
* translating the English *am/are/is ... -ing*

The present tense is formed by adding the present tense endings to the **stem.** The **stem** is the part of the infinitive which is left when the final letters have been removed. The endings vary according to which group the verb belongs to.

    travaill/er   **fin**/ir   **répond**/re

The **Perfect Tense** is used
* in conversation/letters to describe an action in the past which has been completed
* for an action in the past which happened on one occasion only

It is formed by using the present tense of the auxiliary verbs **avoir** or **être** with the past participle of the verb you are using. See Past Participle, page 5.

    j'ai travaillé   **je suis allé(e)**   **je me suis assis(e)**
    I worked   *I went*   *I sat down*

Many verbs have irregular past participles and the common ones are included in the irregular verb tables in Section 3, pages 29-64.

Past participles of the verbs which take **avoir** do not agree with the subject of the verb: elle a **vu**, ils ont **vu**

The verbs which take **être** in the perfect tense are: – all the reflexive verbs and the following 16 common verbs:

  arriver* descendre* venir* entrer* naître* tomber* retourner* devenir*
  partir* monter*   aller* sortir* mourir* rester*   rentrer*   revenir*

With these verbs the past participle changes its spelling to agree with (match) the subject of the verb. See **aller*** and **s'asseoir*** in the verb tables, pages 29 and 30. It is worth noting that some verbs can use either **avoir** or **être** (page 14).

The **Imperfect Tense** is used for
- describing events, people or feelings in the past
- talking or writing about habitual or continuous actions in the past
- talking or writing about incomplete actions in the past
- reported speech
- translating the English *was/were … -ing*

It is formed from the **nous** form of the present tense with the imperfect endings:

> **-ais   -ais   -ait   -ions   -iez   -aient**

nous travaillons	>	travaill + *ending*	>	je travaill**ais**
nous finissons	>	finiss + *ending*	>	je finiss**ais**
nous répondons	>	répond + *ending*	>	je répond**ais**

The **Imperative** is used
- to give a command, to tell someone to do something, or not to do something, to give advice, or to express a wish

The **tu, nous** and **vous** forms are used as appropriate:
- **Tu** is used to one person you know well - a member of your family, a child or a pet.
- **Nous** is used to translate the English *"Let's do something, let's go somewhere"*
- **Vous** is used for one or more adults you do not know well, or two or more people you do know well, or who are members of your family, children or pets.

For **-ir** and **-re** verbs the imperative is formed by using the **tu, nous** and **vous** forms of the present tense without the subject pronouns:

tu réponds	>	**réponds!**	tu finis	> **finis!**
nous répondons	>	**répondons!**	nous finissons	> **finissons!**
vous répondez	>	**répondez!**	vous finissez	> **finissez!**

For **-er** verbs and **aller*** the **nous** and **vous** forms follow the same pattern. The **tu** form, however, drops the final **s**.

tu travailles	>	**travaille!**	tu vas	>	**va!**
nous travaillons	>	**travaillons!**	nous allons	>	**allons!**
vous travaillez	>	**travaillez!**	vous allez	>	**allez!**

Reflexive verbs have two command forms, one positive and one negative.
The pronoun position and form differ, but the verb follows the usual rules.

lave-**toi**!	ne **te** lave pas!
lavons-**nous**!	ne **nous** lavons pas!
lavez-**vous**!	ne **vous** lavez pas!

The **Future Tense** is used
* to talk and write about things which will definitely happen
* to refer to events which will take place in the long term future, rather than the
  immediate future

It is usually formed from the infinitive of the verb with the future tense endings:

          -ai   **-as**   **-a**   **-ons** **-ez**   **-ont**

travailler   >   je travaille**rai**   finir   >   nous fini**rons**

Verbs ending in **-re** drop the final **-e** before adding the future tense endings:

    répondre   >   je répond**rai**

There are many verbs which are irregular in the future and the common ones are
included in the irregular verb tables in Section 3 (pages 29-64).

The **Immediate Future Tense** corresponds to the English *I am going to ...* and is
used
* to talk about events which will take place in the immediate future.

It is formed by using the present tense of **aller** as an auxiliary and the infinitive of
the verb to be put into the future:

    Je **vais partir** bientôt   Ils **vont arriver** aujourd'hui   Elle **va** me **téléphoner**
    I'm going away soon   *They will get here today*   *She is going to phone me*

The **Conditional Tense** is used:
* to express wishes
  Je **voudrais** une pomme   *I would like an apple*
* to write and talk about things you would do if conditions were right
  S'il pleuvait je **resterais** à la maison   Nous **serions** heureux s'il nous téléphonait
  If it rained I would stay at home   *We would be happy if he rang us*

It is formed by using the future stem together with the imperfect endings. It is
given in full wherever possible in the verb tables, but because of lack of space they
may sometimes be printed as below, with the stem in italics for the **je** and **tu** forms,
and the endings only for the rest of the verb:

    je m'*inquiéter*ais   tu t'*inquiéter*ais   il s'---ait   nous nous ---ions, etc.

The **Past Historic Tense** is used in books and newspapers to describe
* a completed action in the past
* a series of events in a story

The Past Historic is **never used in conversation or letters** and is increasingly being replaced in newspapers and modern novels by the less formal perfect tense. It is a tense which you will more often need to recognise rather than use and it is therefore included in the verb tables in its most common forms only, although it does actually have forms for all persons. Many common verbs are irregular in the Past Historic and need to be learned if they are to be recognised easily. The most common irregular forms are listed in the French-English index, pages 65-70.

The **Pluperfect Tense** translates the English *had seen, had gone, had sat down,* etc. It is formed by using the imperfect tense of the auxiliary **avoir** or **être** with the past participle. For rules of agreement see page 5. The pluperfect tense is not printed out in the verb tables, but will always follow one of these three patterns, depending whether the verb takes **avoir** or **être** in the perfect tense.

Verbs with avoir	Verbs with être	Reflexive Verbs
j'avais vu	j'étais allé(e)	je m'étais assis(e)
tu avais vu	tu étais allé(e)	tu t'étais assis(e)
il avait vu	il était allé	il s'était assis
elle avait vu	elle était allée	elle s'était assise
on avait vu	on était allé	on s'était assis
nous avions vu	nous étions allé(e)s	nous nous étions assis(es)
vous aviez vu	vous étiez allé(e)(s)	vous vous étiez assis(e)/(es)
ils avaient vu	ils étaient allés	ils s'étaient assis
elles avaient vu	elles étaient allées	elles s'étaient assises

The key word for the English meaning in the pluperfect tense is **had**, together with the past participle. The examples above translate as follows:

*I **had** seen*	*I **had** gone*	*I **had** sat down*
*I **had** been seeing*	*I **had** been going*	*I **had** been sitting down*, etc

Remember that *have seen* and *saw* are **not** versions of the pluperfect.

The **Past Participle** is the part of a verb used with an auxiliary verb, **avoir** or **être**, to form the Perfect and Pluperfect tenses.

In English the past participle often ends in **-en -ed** or **-t:**

> *given, looked, bought*

In French the past participle ends in **-é -i -u -s** or **-t:**

> donné   fini   répondu   pris   conduit

Many verbs have irregular past participles: **devoir > dû, voir > vu, venir > venu**

When the auxiliary verb is **avoir**, the past participle is usually unchanged, but does sometimes agree with the object if the object comes before the verb in the sentence. This is the **preceding direct object** (PDO).

> la pomme que j'ai cueilli**e**   *the apple which I picked*
> les garçons que j'ai vu**s**   *the boys that I saw*
> les fleurs que j'ai cueilli**es**   *the flowers which I picked*

Agreement

When the auxiliary verb is **être**, the past participle has to change its spelling to agree with the subject of the verb.

Past participles show agreement by:

- adding **-e** to show feminine singular agreement   elle est allé**e**
- adding **-s** to show masculine plural agreement   ils sont allé**s**
  unless it already ends in -s, such as **mis, assis**, when they do not add an extra **-s**.
  A mixed group of plural feminine and masculine is treated as masculine plural.
- adding **-es** to show feminine plural agreement   elles sont allé**es**
                                                          elles sont assis**es**

Singular or plural?

- **singular** refers to one person or thing only
- **plural** refers to two or more persons or things

Persons of the Verb

There are three persons of the verb. They are either singular or plural.

First person includes the speaker: **je, nous**

Second person is being talked to by the speaker: **tu, vous**

Third person is being talked about: **il, elle, on, ils, elles, Sam, les garçons, les filles, les garçons et les filles**

Subject or Object?

- The **subject** is the person or thing performing the action of the verb:
  > **elle** voit le garçon (*she sees the boy*)
- The **object** of the verb is the person or thing receiving the action of the verb:
  > elle voit **le garçon** (*she sees the boy*)

ENGLISH MEANINGS OF TENSES

There are more forms of each tense in English than there are in French.
Je travaille is the one and only form of the present tense in French, but there are three possible forms in English: *I work, I am working, I do work.* (For *don't*, see Negatives, page 8.) The three English forms are used in a variety of situations whereas, in French, this choice of form does not exist. This is also true of many of the other tenses. As well as meaning *one*, **on** can be used for *we*, and also for *they*, when *they* are unknown people, often in authority (on travaille dur *we/they work hard*).

Present Tense

je travaille	*I work, I am working, I do work*
tu travailles	*you work, you are working, you do work*
il travaille	*he works, he is working, he does work*
elle travaille	*she works, she is working, she does work*
on travaille	*one works, one is working, one does work*
nous travaillons	*we work, we are working, we do work*
vous travaillez	*you work, you are working, you do work*
ils travaillent	*they work, they are working, they do work*
elles travaillent	*they work, they are working, they do work*

Perfect Tense

j'ai travaillé	*I worked, I did work, I have worked*
tu as travaillé	*you worked, you did work, you have worked*
il a travaillé	*he worked, he did work, he has worked*
elle a travaillé	*she worked, she did work, she has worked*
on a travaillé	*one worked, one did work, one has worked*
nous avons travaillé	*we worked, we did work, we have worked*
vous avez travaillé	*you worked, you did work, you have worked*
ils ont travaillé	*they worked, they did work, they have worked*
elles ont travaillé	*they worked, they did work, they have worked*

Imperfect Tense

je travaillais	*I was working, I used to work, I worked*
tu travaillais	*you were working, you used to work, you worked*
il travaillait	*he was working, he used to work, he worked*
elle travaillait	*she was working, she used to work, she worked*
on travaillait	*one was working, one used to work, one worked*
nous travaillions	*we were working, we used to work, we worked*
vous travailliez	*you were working, you used to work, you worked*
ils travaillaient	*they were working, they used to work, they worked*
elles travaillaient	*they were working, they used to work, they worked*

Imperative

Travaille!	*Work!*	Ne travaille pas!	*Don't work!*	(*tu* form)
Travaillons!	*Let's work!*	Ne travaillons pas!	*Let's not work!*	(*nous* form)
Travaillez!	*Work!*	Ne travaillez pas!	*Don't work!*	(*vous* form)

Future Tense

je travaillerai	*I shall/will work, I shall/will be working*
tu travailleras	*you will work, you will be working*
il travaillera	*he will work, he will be working*
elle travaillera	*she will work, she will be working*
on travaillera	*one will work, one will be working*
nous travaillerons	*we shall/will work, we shall/will be working*
vous travaillerez	*you will work, you will be working*
ils travailleront	*they will work, they will be working*
elles travailleront	*they will work, they will be working*

Conditional Tense

je travaillerais	*I would/might work, I would be working*
tu travaillerais	*you would/might work, you would be working*
il travaillerait	*he would/might work, he would be working*
elle travaillerait	*she would/might work, she would be working*
on travaillerait	*one would/might work, one would be working*
nous travaillerions	*we would/might work, we would be working*
vous travailleriez	*you would/might work, you would be working*
ils travailleraient	*they would/might work, they would be working*
elles travailleraient	*they would/might work, they would be working*

The Past Historic Tense

il/elle travailla	*he/she worked, he/she did work*
ils/elles travaillèrent	*they worked, they did work*

The Pluperfect Tense

j'avais travaillé	*I had worked, I had been working*
tu avais travaillé	*you had worked, you had been working*
il avait travaillé	*he had worked, he had been working*
elle avait travaillé	*she had worked, she had been working*
on avait travaillé	*one had worked, one had been working*
nous avions travaillé	*we had worked, we had been working*
vous aviez travaillé	*you had worked, you had been working*
ils avaient travaillé	*they had worked, they had been working*
elles avaient travaillé	*they had worked, they had been working*

NEGATIVES

Negatives are the words put with a verb to change its meaning; it then says that something will *not/never/no longer* happen.

In French, negatives usually have two parts - **ne** and another word which varies according to meaning.

ne ... pas	*not*	ne ... personne	*nobody*
ne ... jamais	*never*	ne ... que	*only*
ne ... rien	*nothing*	ne ... ni ... ni	*neither ... nor*
ne ... plus	*no longer*	ne ... nulle part	*nowhere*
		ne ... aucun(e)	*no, not one*

Word order with Negatives

- The general rule is that in simple (one-word) tenses such as the present, future and imperfect tenses **ne** comes before the verb and the **pas/jamais/plus,** etc follows.

Je **ne** regarde **pas** la télévision	*I don't watch television*
Je **ne** regarde **jamais** la télévision	*I never watch television*
Je **ne** regarde **plus** la télévision	*I don't watch television any more*

- When a negative is used with the perfect or pluperfect tense, the position of the second part of the negative varies according to which negative is being used. With **ne ... pas, ne ... jamais, ne ... rien**, and **ne ... plus** the second part of the negative comes *before* the past participle:

Je n'ai **pas** vu le film	*I did not see the film*
Je n'ai **jamais** visité la France	*I have never been to France*
Je n'ai **rien** mangé hier	*I did not eat anything yesterday*
Je n'y ai **plus** pensé	*I did not think about it any more*

But in these examples, the second part follows the past participle:

Je n'ai vu **personne**	*I didn't see anyone*
Je ne suis arrivé **que** lundi	*I only arrived on Monday*
Il n'a eu **ni** ami **ni** ennemi	*He had neither friend nor enemy*
Je ne l'ai vu **nulle part**	*I didn't see him anywhere*
Il n'a eu **aucun** problème	*He had no problem*
Il n'a eu **aucune** idée	*He had no idea*

- When a reflexive verb is negative, the reflexive pronoun follows the **ne**:

Je ne **me** lève pas tôt le matin	*I don't get up early in the morning*
Il ne **s'**est pas couché tard	*He didn't go to bed late*

QUESTION FORMS

Formation of Questions

Questions are also known as Interrogatives.
There are five ways of asking questions in French:

- In speaking, a rising tone of voice can turn a statement into a question:
  > Vous aimez le fromage?
  > *You like cheese?*

- By putting **n'est-ce pas** at the end of a sentence:
  > Il fait froid, **n'est-ce pas**?   Ils sont grands, **n'est-ce pas**?
  > *It's cold, isn't it?*   *They are tall, aren't they?*

- By writing or saying **est-ce que** or **est-ce qu'** at the beginning of the sentence:
  > **Est-ce que** vous aimez le fromage?   **Est-ce qu'**elle aime le fromage?
  > *Do you like cheese?*   *Does she like cheese?*

- By inverting the subject and verb:
  > (When a verb is inverted, the subject is attached to its verb with a hyphen.)
  > **Aimes-tu** le fromage?
  > *Do you like cheese?*
  > When a verb has a vowel as its ending, an extra **-t-** is needed for ease of pronunciation:
  > Ton frère, joue-**t**-il au football?
  > *Does your brother play football?*

- By using a question word at the beginning of the sentence and inverting the verb:
  > **Où** vas-tu passer les vacances de Pâques?
  > ***Where** are you going to spend the Easter holidays?*

Some common question words are:

Combien (de)?	*How much? How many?*
Comment?	*How? What? What is ... like?*
D'où?	*Where from?*
Pourquoi?	*Why?*
Quand?	*When?*
Qu'est-ce que?	*What?*
Quel, Quelle, Quels, Quelles?	*Which?***
Qui?	*Who?*
Quoi?	*What?*
(De quoi parles-tu?)	*(What are you talking about?)*

** These are adjectives and must agree with their noun

TWO VERBS USED TOGETHER

In French the modal verbs **devoir, pouvoir, savoir** and **vouloir** need a second verb
to follow them in the sentence.
This second verb is always put in the infinitive.

je dois **partir**	nous pouvons **partir** demain	il sait **nager**	je voudrais y **aller**
I have to leave	*we can leave tomorrow*	*he can swim*	*I'd like to go there*

This rule also applies when using **aller** to form the **Immediate Future** tense.

il va **acheter** une voiture neuve   *he is going to buy a new car*

There are many other circumstances in which a second verb (in the infinitive) is
required. The infinitive may either be placed straight after the first verb, or it may
require **à** or **de.**
Unfortunately, there is no easy way of knowing which method is used.
The verbs just have to be learned individually with the appropriate preposition.

Some common verbs which are followed directly by an infinitive and need **no
preposition** include:

adorer	elle adore danser	*she loves dancing*
aimer	il aime jouer au golf	*he loves playing golf*
compter	il compte venir bientôt	*he intends coming soon*
désirer	elle désire y aller	*she wants to go there*
détester	il déteste conduire	*he hates driving*
espérer	j'espère y aller	*I hope to go there*
il faut	il faut faire attention	*you must be careful*
penser	elle pense venir bientôt	*she intends to come soon*
préférer	je préfère y aller à pied	*I prefer to walk there*

Some common verbs which require **à** before the infinitive are:

apprendre à	j'apprends **à** conduire	*I am learning to drive*
commencer à	elle commence **à** pleurer	*she starts crying*
continuer à	tu continues **à** travailler	*you go on working*
demander à	il demande **à** sortir	*he asks to go out*
hésiter à	j'hésite **à** y entrer	*I hesitate to go in there*
s'intéresser à	je m'intéresse **à** la musique	*I am interested in music*
jouer à (*sport*)	elle joue **au** tennis	*she plays tennis*
se mettre à	je me mets **à** chanter	*I begin to sing*
passer son temps à	il passe son temps **à** lire	*he spends his time reading*
penser à	je pense **à** mes amis	*I'm thinking about my friends*
ressembler à	tu ressembles **à** ton père	*you are like your father*
réussir à	il a réussi **à** le trouver	*he succeeded in finding it*
téléphoner à	je téléphone **à** ma mère	*I ring my mother*

Some common verbs which require **de** before the infinitive are:

s'arrêter de	il s'arrête **de** grogner	*he stops grumbling*
cesser de	elle a cessé **d'**écrire	*she has stopped writing*
décider de	elle décide **de** m'écrire	*she decides to write to me*
se dépêcher de	je me dépêche **de** le trouver	*I hurry to find him/it*
dire de	je lui dis **de** se dépêcher	*I tell him to hurry up*
essayer de	j'ai essayé **de** te téléphoner	*I tried to phone you*
finir de	il finit **de** manger	*he finishes eating*
jouer de (*instrument*)	il joue **de** la guitare	*he plays the guitar*
oublier de	j'ai oublié **de** lui écrire	*I forgot to write to her/him*
penser de	Que penses-tu **de** lui?	*What do you think of him?*
permettre de	il m'a permis **de** parler	*he allowed me to speak*
refuser de	elle a refusé **de** leur parler	*she refused to speak to them*
regretter de	je regrette **de** te dire que …	*I am sorry to tell you that …*
se souvenir de	elle se souvient **de** ses amis	*she remembers her friends*

No preposition is needed after these verbs in French, even though a preposition is needed in English:

attendre	j'attends le train	*I wait for the train*
chercher	je cherche les enfants	*I am looking for the children*
craindre	je crains l'avenir	*I'm afraid of the future*
écouter	j'écoute la radio	*I listen to the radio*
payer	nous payons les billets	*we pay for the tickets*
regarder	je regarde les animaux	*I look at the animals*
sentir	ça sent la lavande	*it smells of lavender*

SECTION 2 - REGULAR VERBS

There are three main groups of regular verbs.
Each one is known by the last two letters of its infinitive: -**er,** -**ir,** or -**re**

REGULAR -ER VERBS

This is the largest group of regular verbs and it is still growing! New verbs which come into the language usually join this group. They all follow this pattern:

travailler - to work		for English tense meanings see pages 6 and 7	
Impératif *Imperative*	*Présent* *Present*	*Passé composé* *Perfect*	
travaille!	je travaille	j'ai travaillé	
	tu travailles	tu as travaillé	
	il travaille	il a travaillé	
	elle travaille	elle travaillé	
	on travaille	on a travaillé	
travaillons!	nous travaillons	nous avons travaillé	
travaillez!	vous travaillez	vous avez travaillé	
	ils travaillent	ils ont travaillé	
	elles travaillent	elles ont travaillé	
Imparfait *Imperfect*	*Futur* *Future*	*Conditionnel* *Conditional*	*Passé simple* *Past Historic*
je travaillais	je travaillerai	je *travaille*rais	
tu travaillais	tu travailleras	tu *travaille*rais	
il/elle/on travaillait	il/elle/on travaillera	il/elle/on ---ait	il/elle/on travailla
nous travaillions	nous travaillerons	nous ---ions	
vous travailliez	vous travaillerez	vous ---iez	
ils/elles travaillaient	ils/elles travailleront	ils/elles ---aient	ils/elles travaillèrent

There are literally thousands of regular **-er** verbs which follow the pattern of **travailler**. For convenience the most frequently occurring ones have been divided into lists opposite.

Very common regular -er verbs: (for meanings of verbs see **pages 65-70**)

chercher, décider, demander, détester, discuter, donner, fermer, gagner, jouer, laisser, louer, marcher, parler, penser, porter, préparer, regarder, téléphoner, toucher, trouver, visiter

Other common regular -er verbs: (for meanings of verbs see **pages 65-70**)

bavarder, blesser, bricoler, briller, brûler, cacher, casser, causer, cesser, chanter, collectionner, coller, commander, compter, conseiller, continuer, couler, couper, coûter, crier, danser, déclarer, déjeuner, demeurer, dépenser, désirer, dessiner, deviner, dîner, durer, faxer, frapper, fréquenter, fumer, garder, glisser, goûter, grogner, laver, manquer, montrer, passer, photocopier, pleurer, plier, polluer, poser, pousser, prêter, proposer, quitter, raconter, ramasser, recycler, refuser, regretter, remarquer, remercier, rencontrer, renverser, réparer, repasser, réserver, ressembler, réveiller, rouler, sauter, sembler, sonner, télécopier, tirer, tourner, traverser, verser, voler.

Less common -er verbs: (for meanings of verbs see **pages 65-70**)

calculer, camper, communiquer, cultiver, doubler, fatiguer, gronder, guider, manifester, nommer, noter, persuader, piquer, pratiquer, présenter, protester, prouver, râler, redoubler, répliquer, respirer, rêver, rigoler, risquer, saluer, séparer, serrer, soigner, souffler, soupçonner, soupirer, supporter, supposer, surveiller, témoigner, terminer, tousser, trembler, troubler, tuer, vérifier, vider, voter

Regular -er verbs which begin with a vowel or a silent h:
These shorten **je** to **j'**.

Common regular -er verbs which begin with a vowel or silent h:
                              (for meanings of verbs see **pages 65-70**)

accepter, accompagner, admirer, adorer, aider, aimer, allumer, amuser, apporter, approcher, écouter, embrasser, emporter, emprunter, enregistrer, étudier, expliquer, habiter, hésiter, imaginer, informer, inviter, oublier, utiliser.

Less common regular -er verbs which begin with a vowel or silent h:
                              (for meanings of verbs see **pages 65-70**)

abandonner, abîmer, accrocher, adopter, agiter, ajouter, arracher, arrêter, assister, attraper, avaler, éclater, écraser, embarrasser, enseigner, épouser, éviter, exister, exprimer, imiter, indiquer, inventer, irriter, opposer

Regular -er verbs with être   (for meanings of verbs see **pages 65-70**)

- The regular verbs **arriver*, entrer*, monter*, rentrer*, rester*, retourner*** and **tomber*** follow the *travailler* pattern, but they take **être** in the perfect tense. This means that the past participle has to agree with the subject (see page 5).

il est arrivé	*but*	elle est arrivé**e**	*he/she arrived*
ils sont entré**s**	*but*	elles sont entré**es**	*they went in*

monter* - to go up   for English tense meanings see pages 6 and 7

Impératif / Imperative	Présent / Present	Passé composé / Perfect	
monte!	je monte	je suis monté(e)	
	tu montes	tu es monté(e)	
	il monte	il est monté	
	elle monte	elle est montée	
	on monte	on est monté	
montons!	nous montons	nous sommes monté(e)s	
montez!	vous montez	vous êtes monté(e)(s)	
	ils montent	ils sont montés	
	elles montent	elles sont montées	

Imparfait / Imperfect	Futur / Future	Conditionnel / Conditional	Passé simple / Past Historic
je montais	je monterai	je *monter*ais	
tu montais	tu monteras	tu *monter*ais	
il/elle/on montait	il/elle/on montera	il/elle/on ---ait	il/elle/on monta
nous montions	nous monterons	nous ---ions	
vous montiez	vous monterez	vous ---iez	
ils/elles montaient	ils/elles monteront	ils/elles ---aient	ils/elles montèrent

However, **monter**, **rentrer** and **retourner** will take **avoir** if they have a direct object. In this situation the verb behaves like any other verb taking **avoir**.

il/elle/on **a** monté la valise	*he/she/they carried the case upstairs*
ils/elles **ont** monté les valises	*they carried the cases upstairs*
il/elle/on **a** rentré les provisions	*he/she/they brought the groceries in*
ils/elles **ont** rentré les provisions	*they brought the groceries in*
il/elle/on **a** retourné le questionnaire	*he/she/they sent back the questionnaire*
ils/elles **ont** retourné le questionnaire	*they sent back the questionnaire*

REFLEXIVE VERBS

Reflexive verbs are those which have **se** or **s'** in the infinitive. They all take **être** in the perfect tense. Many of these verbs belong to the -**er** group.

In genuinely reflexive verbs, the person or thing receiving the action of the verb is also the person performing the action of the verb:
  je **me** lave *I wash **myself***

This type of verb is also used sometimes when two or more people perform the action of the verb reciprocally (to or for each other):
  Jean et Michel **se** sont rencontrés hier
  *Jean and Michel met **each other** yesterday*

In the perfect tense **te** and **se** are shortened to **t'** and **s'** when followed by a vowel.

se laver* - to wash oneself, to get washed for English tense meanings see pages 6 and 7		
Impératif / **Imperative**	**Présent** / **Present**	**Passé composé** / **Perfect**
	je **me** lave	je **me** suis lavé(e)
lave-**toi**!	tu **te** laves	tu **t'**es lavé(e)
	il **se** lave	il **s'**est lavé
	elle **se** lave	elle **s'**est lavée
	on **se** lave	on **s'**est lavé
lavons-**nous**!	nous **nous** lavons	nous **nous** sommes lavé(e)s
lavez-**vous**!	vous **vous** lavez	vous **vous** êtes lavé(e)(s)
	ils **se** lavent	ils **se** sont lavés
	elles **se** lavent	elles **se** sont lavées

Imparfait / **Imperfect**	**Futur** / **Future**	**Conditionnel** / **Conditional**	**Passé simple** / **Past Historic**
je **me** lavais	je **me** laverai	je **me** *laver*ais	
tu **te** lavais	tu **te** laveras	tu **te** *laver*ais	
il/elle/on **se** lavait	il/elle/on **se** lavera	il/elle/on **se** ---ait	il/elle/on **se** lava
nous **nous** lavions	nous **nous** laverons	nous **nous** ---ions	
vous **vous** laviez	vous **vous** laverez	vous **vous** ---iez	
ils/elles **se** lavaient	ils/elles **se** laveront	ils/elles **se** ---aient	ils/elles **se** lavèrent

Some other commonly used -er reflexive verbs are:
se baigner*, se balader*, se blesser*, se brosser* (les cheveux), se bronzer*, se cacher*, se casser* (le bras, etc), se coucher*, se couper* (le doigt, etc), se débrouiller*, se demander*, se dépêcher*, se déshabiller*, se disputer* avec, se fâcher*, se maquiller*, se passer*, se peigner*, se raser*, se renseigner*, se reposer*, se réveiller*, se sauver*, se trouver*.

When the reflexive verb begins with a **vowel** or **silent h**, the reflexive pronouns **me te** and **se** are shortened to **m'**, **t'** and **s'**.

s'habiller* - to get dressed		for English tense meanings see pages 6 and 7

Impératif Imperative	Présent Present	Passé composé Perfect
habille-toi!	je **m'**habille	je me suis habillé(e)
	tu **t'**habilles	tu **t'**es habillé(e)
	il **s'**habille	il **s'**est habillé
	elle **s'**habille	elle **s'**est habillée
	on **s'**habille	on **s'**est habillé
habillons-nous!	nous nous habillons	nous nous sommes habillé(e)s
habillez-vous!	vous vous habillez	vous vous êtes habillé(e)(s)
	ils **s'**habillent	ils se sont habillés
	elles **s'**habillent	elles se sont habillées

Imparfait Imperfect	Futur Future	Conditionnel Conditional	Passé simple Past Historic
je **m'**habillais	je **m'**habillerai	je **m'***habiller*ais	
tu **t'**habillais	tu **t'**habilleras	tu **t'***habiller*ais	
il/elle/on **s'**habillait	il/elle/on **s'**habillera	il/elle/on **s'**---ait	il/elle/on **s'**habilla
nous nous habillions	nous nous habillerons	nous nous ---ions	
vous vous habilliez	vous vous habillerez	vous vous ---iez	
ils/elles **s'**habillaient	ils/elles **s'**habilleront	ils/elles **s'**---aient	ils/elles **s'**habillèrent

Other verbs of this type are: s'amuser*, s'approcher* de, s'arrêter*, s'excuser*, s'intéresser* à.

Changes of Meaning

There are some pairs of verbs which change their meaning depending on whether they are used reflexively or non-reflexively. The meanings are related but different. When used reflexively they take **être**; when used non-reflexively they take **avoir**. (Remember an * means that the verb takes **être**.)

s'allonger* *to lie down, to grow (child)*	allonger *to make longer*
s'arrêter* *to stop*	arrêter *to arrest*
se conduire* *to behave*	conduire *to drive a vehicle*
se demander* *to wonder*	demander *to ask*
s'ennuyer* *to be bored*	ennuyer *to bore, to worry, to annoy*
se lever* *to get up*	lever *to lift*
se promener* *to go for a walk*	promener *to take for a walk (eg dog)*
se rappeler* *to remember*	rappeler *to remind someone else, to call back*
se rendre* *to surrender*	rendre *to give back, return*
se sentir* *to feel (ill, better)*	sentir *to smell*
se tenir* *to stand*	tenir *to hold*
se trouver* *to be situated*	trouver *to find*

-ER VERBS WHICH HAVE VARIATIONS FROM THE USUAL PATTERN

Some **-er** verbs have variations from the standard pattern. These need to be learned.

- **Commencer** and other verbs ending in **-cer** need a cedilla under the **c** (ç) in parts of the verb where the **c** comes before the hard vowels **a, o** or **u:**

commencer - to begin, to start		for English tense meanings see pages 6 and 7
	Présent / Present	*Passé composé* / Perfect
commence!	je commence	j'ai commencé
	tu commences	tu as commencé
	il commence	il a commencé
	elle commence	elle a commencé
	on commence	on a commencé
commençons!	nous commençons	nous avons commencé
commencez!	vous commencez	vous avez commencé
	ils commencent	ils ont commencé
	elles commencent	elles ont commencé

Imparfait / Imperfect	*Futur* / Future	*Conditionnel* / Conditional	*Passé simple* / Past Historic
je commençais	je commencerai	je *commencer*ais	
tu commençais	tu commenceras	tu *commencer*ais	
il/elle/on commençait	il/elle/on commencera	il/elle/on ---ait	il/elle/on commença
nous commencions	nous commencerons	nous ---ions	
vous commenciez	vous commencerez	vous ---iez	
ils/elles commençaient	ils/elles commenceront	ils/elles ---aient	ils commencèrent

Other verbs of this type are:

coincer, déplacer, divorcer, froncer les sourcils, grincer, lancer, menacer, percer, pincer, placer, prononcer, recommencer, remplacer, renforcer, renoncer, sucer, tracer.

Je is shortened to **j'** if the verb begins with a vowel.
Verbs of this type are: agacer, annoncer, avancer, effacer, enfoncer, exercer.

- **Changer** and other verbs whose infinitive ends in **-ger** need an extra **e** to soften the **g** in parts of the verb where the **g** would otherwise come before the hard vowels **a, o** or **u:**

changer - to change		for English tense meanings see pages 6 and 7
Impératif / *Imperative*	*Présent* / *Present*	*Passé composé* / *Perfect*
change!	je change	j'ai changé
	tu changes	tu as changé
	il change	il a changé
	elle change	elle a changé
	on change	on a changé
changeons!	nous changeons	nous avons changé
changez!	vous changez	vous avez changé
	ils changent	ils ont changé
	elles changent	elles ont changé

Imparfait / *Imperfect*	*Futur* / *Future*	*Conditionnel* / *Conditional*	*Passé simple* / *Past Historic*
je changeais	je changerai	je *changer*ais	
tu changeais	tu changeras	tu *changer*ais	
il/elle/on changeait	il/elle/on changera	il/elle/on ---ait	il/elle/on changea
nous changions	nous changerons	nous ---ions	
vous changiez	vous changerez	vous ---iez	
ils/elles changeaient	ils/elles changeront	ils/elles ---aient	ils/elles changèrent

Other verbs of this type are:

bouger, charger, corriger, déménager, déranger, juger, loger, longer, manger, mélanger, nager, négliger, neiger, partager, piger, plonger, prolonger, rager, rallonger, ranger, rédiger, ronger, songer, soulager, venger, voyager.

Je is shortened to **j'** if the verb begins with a vowel or silent **h.**
Verbs of this type are: affliger, allonger, aménager, arranger, échanger, encourager, exiger, héberger, interroger, obliger.

S'allonger*, se diriger*, s'engager*, being reflexive, take **être** in the perfect tense.

Protéger is unusual because not only does it need the extra **-e** before the hard vowels **a**, **o** or **u** to keep the **g** soft, but it also changes the **é** to **è** before a silent final **e**.

protéger - to protect		for English tense meanings see pages 6 and 7
Impératif *Imperative*	*Présent* *Present*	*Passé composé* *Perfect*
	je protège	j'ai protégé
protège!	tu protèges	tu as protégé
	il protège	il a protégé
	elle protège	elle a protégé
	on protège	on a protégé
protégeons!	nous protégeons	nous avons protégé
protégez!	vous protégez	vous avez protégé
	ils protègent	ils ont protégé
	elles protègent	elles ont protégé

Imparfait *Imperfect*	*Futur* *Future*	*Conditionnel* *Conditional*	*Passé simple* *Past Historic*
je protégeais	je protégerai	je *protéger*ais	
tu protégeais	tu protégeras	tu *protéger*ais	
il/elle/on protégeait	il/elle/on protégera	il/elle/on ---ait	il/elle/on protégea
nous protégions	nous protégerons	nous ---ions	
vous protégiez	vous protégerez	vous ---iez	
ils/elles protégeaient	ils/elles protégeront	ils/elles ---aient	ils/elles protégèrent

- **Jeter** doubles the **t** before a silent or unstressed final **-e**.

jeter - to throw		for English tense meanings see pages 6 and 7
Impératif *Imperative*	*Présent* *Present*	*Passé composé* *Perfect*
	je jette	j'ai jeté
jette!	tu jettes	tu as jeté
	il/elle/on jette	il/elle/on a jeté
	nous jetons	nous avons jeté
jetons!	vous jetez	vous avez jeté
jetez!	ils jettent	ils ont jeté
	elles jettent	elles ont jeté

Imparfait *Imperfect*	*Futur* *Future*	*Conditionnel* *Conditional*	*Passé simple* *Past Historic*
je jetais	je jetterai	je jetterais	
tu jetais	tu jetteras	tu jetterais	
il/elle/on jetait	il/elle/on jettera	il/elle/on jetterait	il/elle/on jeta
nous jetions	nous jetterons	nous jetterions	
vous jetiez	vous jetterez	vous jetteriez	
ils/elles jetaient	ils/elles jetteront	ils/elles jetteraient	ils/elles jetèrent

• **Appeler** and **rappeler** double the **l** before a silent or unstressed final-**e**.

appeler - to call		for English tense meanings see pages 6 and 7

Impératif Imperative	Présent Present	Passé composé Perfect	
	j'appelle	j'ai appelé	
appelle!	tu appelles	tu as appelé	
	il appelle	il a appelé	
	elle appelle	elle a appelé	
	on appelle	on a appelé	
appelons!	nous appelons	nous avons appelé	
appelez!	vous appelez	vous avez appelé	
	ils appellent	ils ont appelé	
	elles appellent	elles ont appelé	
Imparfait **Imperfect**	**Futur** **Future**	**Conditionnel** **Conditional**	**Passé simple** **Past Historic**
j'appelais	j'appellerai	j'*appeller*ais	
tu appelais	tu appelleras	tu *appeller*ais	
il/elle/on appelait	il/elle/on appellera	il/elle/on ---ait	il/elle/on appela
nous appelions	nous appellerons	nous ---ions	
vous appeliez	vous appellerez	vous ---iez	
ils/elles appelaient	ils/elles appelleront	ils/elles ---aient	ils/elles appelèrent

S'appeler* and **se rappeler***, being reflexive verbs, take **être** in the perfect tense

s'appeler* - to be called		for English tense meanings see pages 6 and 7

Impératif Imperative	Présent Present	Passé composé Perfect	
	je m'appelle	je me suis appelé(e)	
appelle-toi!	tu t'appelles	tu t'es appelé(e)	
	il s'appelle	il s'est appelé	
	elle s'appelle	elle s'est appelée	
	on s'appelle	on s'est appelé	
appelons-nous!	nous nous appelons	nous nous sommes appelé(e)s	
appelez-vous!	vous vous appelez	vous vous êtes appelé(e)(s)	
	ils s'appellent	ils se sont appelés	
	elles s'appellent	elles se sont appelées	
Imparfait **Imperfect**	**Futur** **Future**	**Conditionnel** **Conditional**	**Passé simple** **Past Historic**
je m'appelais	je m'appellerai	je m'*appeller*ais	
tu t'appelais	tu t'appelleras	tu t'*appeller*ais	
il/elle/on s'appelait	il/elle/on s'appellera	il/elle/on s'---ait	il/elle/on s'appela
nous nous appelions	nous nous appellerons	nous nous ---ions	
vous vous appeliez	vous vous appellerez	vous vous ---iez	
ils/elles s'appelaient	ils/elles s'appelleront	ils/elles s'---aient	ils/elles s'appelèrent

- Verbs ending **e-consonant-er** (except appeler, page 20 and jeter, page 19) add an accent when the final **-e** is silent or unstressed.

acheter - to buy		for English tense meanings see pages 6 and 7
Impératif / *Imperative*	*Présent* / *Present*	*Passé composé* / *Perfect*
	j'achète	j'ai acheté
achète!	tu achètes	tu as acheté
	il/elle achète	il/elle a acheté
	on achète	on a acheté
achetons!	nous achetons	nous avons acheté
achetez!	vous achetez	vous avez acheté
	ils achètent	ils ont acheté
	elles achètent	elles ont acheté

Imparfait / *Imperfect*	*Futur* / *Future*	*Conditionnel* / *Conditional*	*Passé simple* / *Past Historic*
j'achetais	j'achèterai	j'*achèter*ais	
tu achetais	tu achèteras	tu *achèter*ais	
il/elle/on achetait	il/elle/on achètera	il/elle/on ---ait	il/elle/on acheta
nous achetions	nous achèterons	nous ---ions	
vous achetiez	vous achèterez	vous ---iez	
ils/elles achetaient	ils/elles achèteront	ils/elles ---aient	ils/elles achetèrent

Other verbs of this type are: achever, amener, emmener, enlever, geler, lever, mener, peser, promener, ramener

Se lever* and **se promener*,** being reflexive, take **être** in the perfect tense.

se lever* - to get up, to stand up		for English tense meanings see pages 6 and 7
Impératif / *Imperative*	*Présent* / *Present*	*Passé composé* / *Perfect*
	je me lève	je me suis levé(e)
lève-toi!	tu te lèves	tu t'es levé(e)
	il se lève	il s'est levé
	elle se lève	elle s'est levée
	on se lève	on s'est levé
levons-nous!	nous nous levons	nous nous sommes levé(e)s
levez-vous!	vous vous levez	vous vous êtes levé(e)(s)
	ils se lèvent	ils se sont levés
	elles se lèvent	elles se sont levées

Imparfait / *Imperfect*	*Futur* / *Future*	*Conditionnel* / *Conditional*	*Passé simple* / *Past Historic*
je me levais	je me lèverai	je me *lèver*ais	
tu te levais	tu te lèveras	tu te *lèver*ais	
il/elle/on se levait	il/elle/on se lèvera	il/elle/on se ---ait	il/elle/on se leva
nous nous levions	nous nous lèverons	nous nous ---ions	
vous vous leviez	vous vous lèverez	vous vous ---iez	
ils/elles se levaient	ils/elles se lèveront	ils/elles se ---aient	ils/elles se levèrent

- Verbs ending in **é-consonant-er** change the **é** to **è** before a silent final **-e**.

préférer - to prefer, to like … better   for English tense meanings see pages 6 and 7

Impératif *Imperative*	*Présent* *Present*	*Passé composé* *Perfect*	
	je préfère	j'ai préféré	
préfère!	tu préfères	tu as préféré	
	il/elle/on préfère	il/elle/on a préféré	
préférons!	nous préférons	nous avons préféré	
préférez!	vous préférez	vous avez préféré	
	ils préfèrent	ils ont préféré	
	elles préfèrent	elles ont préféré	

Imparfait *Imperfect*	*Futur* *Future*	*Conditionnel* *Conditional*	*Passé simple* *Past Historic*
je préférais	je préférerai	je *préférer*ais	
tu préférais	tu préféreras	tu *préférer*ais	
il/elle/on préférait	il/elle/on préférera	il/elle/on ---ait	il/elle/on préféra
nous préférions	nous préférerons	nous ---ions	
vous préfériez	vous préférerez	vous ---iez	
ils/elles préféraient	ils/elles préféreront	ils/elles ---aient	ils/elles préférèrent

Other verbs of this type are: accélérer, céder, compléter, considérer, espérer, exagérer, inquiéter, posséder, régler, répéter, révéler, suggérer.

S'inquiéter*, being reflexive, takes **être** in the perfect tense.

s'inquiéter* - to worry   for English tense meanings see pages 6 and 7

Impératif *Imperative*	*Présent* *Present*	*Passé composé* *Perfect*	
	je m'inquiète	je me suis inquiété(e)	
ne t'inquiète pas!	tu t'inquiètes	tu t'es inquiété(e)	
	il s'inquiète	il s'est inquiété	
	elle s'inquiète	elle s'est inquiétée	
	on s'inquiète	on s'est inquiété	
ne nous inquiétons pas	nous nous inquiétons	nous nous sommes inquiété(e)s	
ne vous inquiétez pas!	vous vous inquiétez	vous vous êtes inquiété(e)(s)	
	ils s'inquiètent	ils se sont inquiétés	
	elles s'inquiètent	elles se sont inquiétées	

Imparfait *Imperfect*	*Futur* *Future*	*Conditionnel* *Conditional*	*Passé simple* *Past Historic*
je m'inquiétais	je m'inquiéterai	je m'*inquiéter*ais	
tu t'inquiétais	tu t'inquiéteras	tu t'*inquiéter*ais	
il/elle/on s'inquiétait	il/elle/on s'inquiétera	il/elle/on s'---ait	il/elle/on s'inquiéta
nous nous inquiétions	nous nous inquiéterons	nous nous ---ions	
vous vous inquiétiez	vous vous inquiéterez	vous vous ---iez	
ils/elles s'inquiétaient	ils/elles s'inquiéteront	ils/elles s'---aient	ils/elles s'inquiétèrent

- Verbs such as **payer** whose infinitive ends in **-ayer** may have two acceptable forms in some tenses. They usually change the **-y** to **-i** before a silent **-e**, but may keep the **-y** throughout. You may also see them with a **-y** (eg je paye).

payer - to pay		for English tense meanings see pages 6 and 7	
Impératif *Imperative*	*Présent* *Present*	*Passé composé* *Perfect*	
	je paie	j'ai payé	
paie!	tu paies	tu as payé	
	il paie	il a payé	
	elle paie	elle a payé	
	on paie	on a payé	
payons!	nous payons	nous avons payé	
payez!	vous payez	vous avez payé	
	ils paient	ils ont payé	
	elles paient	elles ont payé	
Imparfait *Imperfect*	*Futur* *Future*	*Conditionnel* *Conditional*	*Passé simple* *Past Historic*
je payais	je payerai	je payerais	
tu payais	tu payeras	tu payerais	
il/elle/on payait	il/elle/on payera	il/elle/on payerait	il/elle/on paya
nous payions	nous payerons	nous payerions	
vous payiez	vous payerez	vous payeriez	
ils/elles payaient	ils/elles payeront	ils/elles payeraient	ils/elles payèrent

Another verb of this type is: balayer.

Je is shortened to **j'** if the verb begins with a vowel or silent **h**.
A verb of this type is: essayer.

- Verbs whose infinitive ends in -**oyer** and -**uyer** change the -**y** to an -**i** before a silent or unstressed final -**e.**

nettoyer - to clean		for English tense meanings see pages 6 and 7	
Impératif *Imperative*	*Présent* *Present*	*Passé composé* *Perfect*	
nettoie!	je nettoie tu nettoies il nettoie elle nettoie on nettoie	j'ai nettoyé tu as nettoyé il a nettoyé elle a nettoyé on a nettoyé	
nettoyons! nettoyez!	nous nettoyons vous nettoyez ils nettoient elles nettoient	nous avons nettoyé vous avez nettoyé ils ont nettoyé elles ont nettoyé	
Imparfait *Imperfect*	*Futur* *Future*	*Conditionnel* *Conditional*	*Passé simple* *Past Historic*
je nettoyais tu nettoyais il/elle/on nettoyait nous nettoyions vous nettoyiez ils/elles nettoyaient	je nettoierai tu nettoieras il/elle/on nettoiera nous nettoierons vous nettoierez ils/elles nettoieront	je nettoierais tu nettoierais il/elle/on ---ait nous ---ions vous ---iez ils/elles ---aient	il/elle/on nettoya ils/elles nettoyèrent

Je is shortened to **j'** if the verb begins with a vowel or silent **h.**
Other verbs of this type are: aboyer, appuyer, employer, ennuyer, essuyer.

S'ennuyer*, se tutoyer* and se vouvoyer*, being reflexive, take **être** in the perfect tense.

s'ennuyer* - to be bored		for English tense meanings see pages 6 and 7
Impératif / *Imperative*	**Présent** / *Present*	**Passé composé** / *Perfect*
	je m'ennuie	je me suis ennuyé(e)
ne t'ennuie pas!	tu t'ennuies	tu t'es ennuyé(e)
	il s'ennuie	il s'est ennuyé
	elle s'ennuie	elle s'est ennuyée
	on s'ennuie	on s'est ennuyé
ne nous ennuyons pas!	nous nous ennuyons	nous nous sommes ennuyé(e)s
ne vous ennuyez pas!	vous vous ennuyez	vous vous êtes ennuyé(e)(s)
	ils s'ennuient	ils se sont ennuyés
	elles s'ennuient	elles se sont ennuyées

Imparfait / *Imperfect*	**Futur** / *Future*	**Conditionnel** / *Conditional*	**Passé simple** / *Past Historic*
je m'ennuyais	je m'ennuierai	je m'*ennuier*ais	
tu t'ennuyais	tu t'ennuieras	tu t'*ennuier*ais	
il/elle/on s'ennuyait	il/elle/on s'ennuiera	il/elle/on s'---ait	il/elle/on s'ennuya
nous nous ennuyions	nous nous ennuierons	nous nous ---ions	
vous vous ennuyiez	vous vous ennuierez	vous vous ---iez	
ils/elles s'ennuyaient	ils/elles s'ennuieront	ils/elles s'---aient	ils/elles s'ennuyèrent

Envoyer and **renvoyer** are irregular in the future and conditional tenses too.

envoyer - to send		for English tense meanings see pages 6 and 7
Impératif / *Imperative*	**Présent** / *Present*	**Passé composé** / *Perfect*
	j'envoie	j'ai envoyé
envoie!	tu envoies	tu as envoyé
	il envoie	il a envoyé
	elle envoie	elle a envoyé
	on envoie	on a envoyé
envoyons!	nous envoyons	nous avons envoyé
envoyez!	vous envoyez	vous avez envoyé
	ils envoient	ils ont envoyé
	elles envoient	elles ont envoyé

Imparfait / *Imperfect*	**Futur** / *Future*	**Conditionnel** / *Conditional*	**Passé simple** / *Past Historic*
j'envoyais	j'enverrai	j'*enverr*ais	
tu envoyais	tu enverras	tu *enverr*ais	
il/elle/on envoyait	il/elle/on enverra	il/elle/on ---ait	il/elle/on envoya
nous envoyions	nous enverrons	nous ---ions	
vous envoyiez	vous enverrez	vous ---iez	
ils/elles envoyaient	ils/elles enverront	ils/elles ---aient	ils/elles envoyèrent

REGULAR -IR VERBS

The second group of regular verbs is much smaller than the **-er** group. Very few new verbs apart from **alunir** *to land on the moon* have joined this group.

Regular **-ir** verbs follow the pattern shown below.

finir - to finish		for English tense meanings see pages 6 and 7	
Impératif *Imperative*	*Présent* *Present*	*Passé composé* *Perfect*	
finis!	je finis tu finis il finit elle finit on finit	j'ai fini tu as fini il a fini elle a fini on a fini	
finissons! finissez!	nous finissons vous finissez ils finissent elles finissent	nous avons fini vous avez fini ils ont fini elles ont fini	
Imparfait *Imperfect*	*Futur* *Future*	*Conditionnel* *Conditional*	*Passé simple* *Past Historic*
je finissais tu finissais il/elle/on finissait nous finissions vous finissiez ils/elles finissaient	je finirai tu finiras il/elle/on finira nous finirons vous finirez ils/elles finiront	je finirais tu finirais il/elle/on finirait nous finirions vous finiriez ils/elles finiraient	 il/elle/on finit ils/elles finirent

Other common verbs of this type are: bâtir, choisir, démolir, grandir, punir, réfléchir, remplir, réussir, rougir, saisir, vieillir.

Je is shortened to **j'** if the verb begins with a vowel
Verbs of this type are: agrandir, applaudir, atterrir.

-IR VERBS WHICH HAVE VARIATIONS FROM THE USUAL PATTERN

Some **-ir** verbs have variations from the regular pattern.

- The first group of these includes: couvrir, découvrir, offrir, ouvrir, souffrir

- The second group includes: mentir, partir*, sentir, se sentir*, servir, se servir*, sortir* (Verbs marked * take **être** in the perfect tense)

- The third group includes: cueillir, accueillir, recueillir

All of the above verbs except accueillir and recueillir (which are like cueillir) are given in Section 3 in the irregular verb tables. (pages 29-64)

REGULAR -RE VERBS

The third group of regular verbs has an infinitive ending in **-re**. Regular verbs follow the pattern below. No new verbs created to describe new inventions or developments have joined this group.

répondre - to answer		for English tense meanings see pages 6 and 7	
Impératif / *Imperative*	*Présent* / *Present*	*Passé composé* / *Perfect*	
	je réponds	j'ai répondu	
réponds!	tu réponds	tu as répondu	
	il répond	il a répondu	
	elle répond	elle a répondu	
	on répond	on a répondu	
répondons!	nous répondons	nous avons répondu	
répondez!	vous répondez	vous avez répondu	
	ils répondent	ils ont répondu	
	elles répondent	elles ont répondu	
Imparfait / *Imperfect*	*Futur* / *Future*	*Conditionnel* / *Conditional*	*Passé simple* / *Past Historic*
je répondais	je répondrai	je *répondr*ais	
tu répondais	tu répondras	tu *répondr*ais	
il/elle/on répondait	il/elle/on répondra	il/elle/on ---ait	il/elle/on répondit
nous répondions	nous répondrons	nous ---ions	
vous répondiez	vous répondrez	vous ---iez	
ils/elles répondaient	ils/elles répondront	ils/elles ---aient	ils/elles répondirent

Other verbs of this type are: pendre, perdre, rendre, tondre la pelouse, vendre.

Je is shortened to **j'** if the verb begins with a vowel.
Verbs of this type are: attendre, entendre.

Descendre takes **être** in the perfect tense when it does not have a direct object.

descendre* - to go down   for English tense meanings see pages 6 and 7

Impératif / Imperative	Présent / Present	Passé composé / Perfect	
	je descends	je suis descendu(e)	
descends!	tu descends	tu es descendu(e)	
	il descend	il est descendu	
	elle descend	elle est descendue	
	on descend	on est descendu	
descendons!	nous descendons	nous sommes descendu(e)s	
descendez!	vous descendez	vous êtes descendu(e)(s)	
	ils descendent	ils sont descendus	
	elles descendent	elles sont descendues	

Imparfait / Imperfect	Futur / Future	Conditionnel / Conditional	Passé simple / Past Historic
je descendais	je descendrai	je *descend*rais	
tu descendais	tu descendras	tu *descend*rais	
il/elle/on descendait	il/elle/on descendra	il/elle/on ---ait	il/elle/on descendit
nous descendions	nous descendrons	nous ---ions	
vous descendiez	vous descendrez	vous ---iez	
ils/elles descendaient	ils/elles descendront	ils/elles ---aient	ils/elles descendirent

Se rendre*, being reflexive, takes **être**.

se rendre* - to surrender   for English tense meanings see pages 6 and 7

Impératif / Imperative	Présent / Present	Passé composé / Perfect	
	je me rends	je me suis rendu(e)	
rends-toi!	tu te rends	tu t'es rendu(e)	
	il se rend	il s'est rendu	
	elle se rend	elle s'est rendue	
	on se rend	on s'est rendu	
rendons-nous!	nous nous rendons	nous nous sommes rendu(e)s	
rendez-vous!	vous vous rendez	vous vous êtes rendu(e)(s)	
	ils se rendent	ils se sont rendus	
	elles se rendent	elles se sont rendues	

Imparfait / Imperfect	Futur / Future	Conditionnel / Conditional	Passé simple / Past Historic
je me rendais	je me rendrai	je me *rend*rais	
tu te rendais	tu te rendras	tu te *rend*rais	
il/elle/on se rendait	il/elle/on se rendra	il/elle/on se ---ait	il/elle/on se rendit
nous nous rendions	nous nous rendrons	nous nous ---ions	
vous vous rendiez	vous vous rendrez	vous vous ---iez	
ils/elles se rendaient	ils/elles se rendront	ils/elles se ---aient	ils/elles se rendirent

SECTION 3 - IRREGULAR VERBS

aller* - to go		for English tense meanings see pages 6 and 7	
Impératif / *Imperative*	**Présent** / *Present*	**Passé composé** / *Perfect*	
	je vais	je suis allé(e)	
va!	tu vas	tu es allé(e)	
	il va	il est allé	
	elle va	elle est allée	
	on va	on est allé	
allons!	nous allons	nous sommes allé(e)s	
allez!	vous allez	vous êtes allé(e)(s)	
	ils vont	ils sont allés	
	elles vont	elles sont allées	
Imparfait / *Imperfect*	**Futur** / *Future*	**Conditionnel** / *Conditional*	**Passé simple** / *Past Historic*
j'allais	j'irai	j'irais	
tu allais	tu iras	tu irais	
il/elle/on allait	il/elle/on ira	il/elle/on irait	il/elle/on alla
nous allions	nous irons	nous irions	
vous alliez	vous irez	vous iriez	
ils/elles allaient	ils/elles iront	ils/elles iraient	ils/elles allèrent

apprendre - to learn		for English tense meanings see pages 6 and 7	
Impératif / *Imperative*	**Présent** / *Present*	**Passé composé** / *Perfect*	
	j'apprends	j'ai appris	
apprends!	tu apprends	tu as appris	
	il apprend	il a appris	
	elle apprend	elle a appris	
	on apprend	on a appris	
apprenons!	nous apprenons	nous avons appris	
apprenez!	vous apprenez	vous avez appris	
	ils apprennent	ils ont appris	
	elles apprennent	elles ont appris	
Imparfait / *Imperfect*	**Futur** / *Future*	**Conditionnel** / *Conditional*	**Passé simple** / *Past Historic*
j'apprenais	j'apprendrai	j'*apprend*rais	
tu apprenais	tu apprendras	tu *apprend*rais	
il/elle/on apprenait	il/elle/on apprendra	il/elle/on ---ait	il/elle/on apprit
nous apprenions	nous apprendrons	nous ---ions	
vous appreniez	vous apprendrez	vous ---iez	
ils/elles apprenaient	ils/elles apprendront	ils/elles ---aient	ils/elles apprirent

s'asseoir* - to sit down — for English tense meanings see pages 6 and 7

Impératif / Imperative	Présent / Present	Passé composé / Perfect
assieds-toi!	je m'assieds	je me suis assis(e)
	tu t'assieds	tu t'es assis(e)
	il s'assied	il s'est assis
	elle s'assied	elle s'est assise
	on s'assied	on s'est assis
asseyons-nous!	nous nous asseyons	nous nous sommes assis(es)
asseyez-vous!	vous vous asseyez	vous vous êtes assis(e)/(es)
	ils s'asseyent	ils se sont assis
	elles s'asseyent	elles se sont assises

Imparfait / Imperfect	Futur / Future	Conditionnel / Conditional	Passé simple / Past Historic
je m'asseyais	je m'assiérai	je m'*assiér*ais	
tu t'asseyais	tu t'assiéras	tu t'*assiér*ais	
il/elle/on s'asseyait	il/elle/on s'assiéra	il/elle/on s'---ait	il/elle/on s'assit
nous nous asseyions	nous nous assiérons	nous nous --ions	
vous vous asseyiez	vous vous assiérez	vous vous ---iez	
ils/elles s'asseyaient	ils/elles s'assiéront	ils/elles s'---aient	ils/elles s'assirent

avoir - to have — for English tense meanings see pages 6 and 7

Impératif / Imperative	Présent / Present	Passé composé / Perfect
aie!	j'ai	j'ai eu
	tu as	tu as eu
	il a	il a eu
	elle a	elle a eu
	on a	on a eu
ayons!	nous avons	nous avons eu
ayez!	vous avez	vous avez eu
	ils ont	ils ont eu
	elles ont	elles ont eu

Imparfait / Imperfect	Futur / Future	Conditionnel / Conditional	Passé simple / Past Historic
j'avais	j'aurai	j'aurais	
tu avais	tu auras	tu aurais	
il/elle/on avait	il/elle/on aura	il/elle/on aurait	il/elle/on eut
nous avions	nous aurons	nous aurions	
vous aviez	vous aurez	vous auriez	
ils/elles avaient	ils/elles auront	ils/elles auraient	ils/elles eurent

battre - to beat
for English tense meanings see pages 6 and 7

Impératif Imperative	Présent Present	Passé composé Perfect	
	je bats	j'ai battu	
bats!	tu bats	tu as battu	
	il bat	il a battu	
	elle bat	elle a battu	
	on bat	on a battu	
battons!	nous battons	nous avons battu	
battez!	vous battez	vous avez battu	
	ils battent	ils ont battu	
	elles battent	elles ont battu	

Imparfait Imperfect	Futur Future	Conditionnel Conditional	Passé simple Past Historic
je battais	je battrai	je battrais	
tu battais	tu battras	tu battrais	
il/elle/on battait	il/elle/on battra	il/elle/on battrait	il/elle/on battit
nous battions	nous battrons	nous battrions	
vous battiez	vous battrez	vous battriez	
ils/elles battaient	ils/elles battront	ils/elles battraient	ils/elles battirent

boire - to drink
for English tense meanings see pages 6 and 7

Impératif Imperative	Présent Present	Passé composé Perfect	
	je bois	j'ai bu	
bois!	tu bois	tu as bu	
	il boit	il a bu	
	elle boit	elle a bu	
	on boit	on a bu	
buvons!	nous buvons	nous avons bu	
buvez!	vous buvez	vous avez bu	
	ils boivent	ils ont bu	
	elles boivent	elles ont bu	

Imparfait Imperfect	Futur Future	Conditionnel Conditional	Passé simple Past Historic
je buvais	je boirai	je boirais	
tu buvais	tu boiras	tu boirais	
il/elle/on buvait	il/elle/on boira	il/elle/on boirait	il/elle/on but
nous buvions	nous boirons	nous boirions	
vous buviez	vous boirez	vous boiriez	
ils/elles buvaient	ils/elles boiront	ils/elles boiraient	ils/elles burent

comprendre - to understand   for English tense meanings see pages 6 and 7

Impératif / Imperative	Présent / Present	Passé composé / Perfect	
	je comprends	j'ai compris	
comprends!	tu comprends	tu as compris	
	il comprend	il a compris	
	elle comprend	elle a compris	
	on comprend	on a compris	
comprenons!	nous comprenons	nous avons compris	
comprenez!	vous comprenez	vous avez compris	
	ils comprennent	ils ont compris	
	elles comprennent	elles ont compris	

Imparfait / Imperfect	Futur / Future	Conditionnel / Conditional	Passé simple / Past Historic
je comprenais	je comprendrai	je *comprendr*ais	
tu comprenais	tu comprendras	tu *comprendr*ais	
il/elle/on comprenait	il/elle comprendra	il/elle/on ---ait	il/elle/on comprit
nous comprenions	nous comprendrons	nous ---ions	
vous compreniez	vous comprendrez	vous ---iez	
ils/elles comprenaient	ils/elles comprendront	ils/elles ---aient	ils/elles comprirent

conduire - to drive   for English tense meanings see pages 6 and 7

Impératif / Imperative	Présent / Present	Passé composé / Perfect	
	je conduis	j'ai conduit	
conduis!	tu conduis	tu as conduit	
	il conduit	il a conduit	
	elle conduit	elle a conduit	
	on conduit	on a conduit	
conduisons!	nous conduisons	nous avons conduit	
conduisez!	vous conduisez	vous avez conduit	
	ils conduisent	ils ont conduit	
	elles conduisent	elles ont conduit	

Imparfait / Imperfect	Futur / Future	Conditionnel / Conditional	Passé simple / Past Historic
je conduisais	je conduirai	je *conduir*ais	
tu conduisais	tu conduiras	tu *conduir*ais	
il/elle/on conduisait	il/elle/on conduira	il/elle/on ---ait	il/elle/on conduisit
nous conduisions	nous conduirons	nous ---ions	
vous conduisiez	vous conduirez	vous ---iez	
ils/elles conduisaient	ils/elles conduiront	ils/elles ---aient	ils/elles conduisirent

connaître - to know (person, place, film)   for English tense meanings see pages 6 and 7

Impératif Imperative	Présent Present	Passé composé Perfect	
	je connais	j'ai connu	
connais!	tu connais	tu as connu	
	il connaît	il a connu	
	elle connaît	elle a connu	
	on connaît	on a connu	
connaissons!	nous connaissons	nous avons connu	
connaissez!	vous connaissez	vous avez connu	
	ils connaissent	ils ont connu	
	elles connaissent	elles ont connu	

Imparfait Imperfect	Futur Future	Conditionnel Conditional	Passé simple Past Historic
je connaissais	je connaîtrai	je *connaîtr*ais	
tu connaissais	tu connaîtras	tu *connaîtr*ais	
il/elle/on connaissait	il/elle/on connaîtra	il/elle/on ---ait	il/elle/on connut
nous connaissions	nous connaîtrons	nous ---ions	
vous connaissiez	vous connaîtrez	vous ---iez	
ils/elles connaissaient	ils/elles connaîtront	ils/elles ---aient	ils/elles connurent

construire - to build   for English tense meanings see pages 6 and 7

Impératif Imperative	Présent Present	Passé composé Perfect	
	je construis	j'ai construit	
construis!	tu construis	tu as construit	
	il construit	il a construit	
	elle construit	elle a construit	
	on construit	on a construit	
construisons!	nous construisons	nous avons construit	
construisez!	vous construisez	vous avez construit	
	ils construisent	ils ont construit	
	elles construisent	elles ont construit	

Imparfait Imperfect	Futur Future	Conditionnel Conditional	Passé simple Past Historic
je construisais	je construirai	je *construir*ais	
tu construisais	tu construiras	tu *construir*ais	
il/elle construisait	il/elle/on construira	il/elle/on ---ait	il/elle/on construisit
nous construisions	nous construirons	nous ---ions	
vous construisiez	vous construirez	vous ---iez	
ils/elles construisaient	ils/elles construiront	ils/elles ---aient	ils/elles construisirent

contenir - to contain, to hold back — for English tense meanings see pages 6 and 7

Impératif / Imperative	Présent / Present	Passé composé / Perfect
	je contiens	j'ai contenu
contiens!	tu contiens	tu as contenu
	il contient	il contenu
	elle contient	elle a contenu
	on contient	on a contenu
contenons!	nous contenons	nous avons contenu
contenez!	vous contenez	vous avez contenu
	ils contiennent	ils ont contenu
	elles contiennent	elles ont contenu

Imparfait / Imperfect	Futur / Future	Conditionnel / Conditional	Passé simple / Past Historic
je contenais	je contiendrai	je *contiendra*is	
tu contenais	tu contiendras	tu *contiendra*is	
il/elle/on contenait	il/elle/on contiendra	il/elle/on ---ait	il/elle/on contint
nous contenions	nous contiendrons	nous ---ions	
vous conteniez	vous contiendrez	vous ---iez	
ils/elles contenaient	ils/elles contiendront	ils/elles ---aient	ils/elles continrent

coudre - to sew — for English tense meanings see pages 6 and 7

Impératif / Imperative	Présent / Present	Passé composé / Perfect
	je couds	j'ai cousu
couds!	tu couds	tu as cousu
	il coud	il a cousu
	elle coud	elle a cousu
	on coud	on a cousu
cousons!	nous cousons	nous avons cousu
cousez!	vous cousez	vous avez cousu
	ils cousent	ils ont cousu
	elles cousent	elles ont cousu

Imparfait / Imperfect	Futur / Future	Conditionnel / Conditional	Passé simple / Past Historic
je cousais	je coudrai	je coudrais	
tu cousais	tu coudras	tu coudrais	
il/elle/on cousait	il/elle/on coudra	il/elle/on coudrait	il/elle/on cousit
nous cousions	nous coudrons	nous coudrions	
vous cousiez	vous coudrez	vous coudriez	
ils/elles cousaient	ils/elles coudront	ils/elles coudraient	ils/elles cousirent

courir - to run		for English tense meanings see pages 6 and 7
Impératif *Imperative*	*Présent* *Present*	*Passé composé* *Perfect*
	je cours	j'ai couru
cours!	tu cours	tu as couru
	il court	il a couru
	elle court	elle a couru
	on court	on a couru
courons!	nous courons	nous avons couru
courez!	vous courez	vous avez couru
	ils courent	ils ont couru
	elles courent	elles ont couru

Imparfait *Imperfect*	*Futur* *Future*	*Conditionnel* *Conditional*	*Passé simple* *Past Historic*
je courais	je courrai	je courrais	
tu courais	tu courras	tu courrais	
il/elle/on courait	il/elle/on courra	il/elle/on courrait	il/elle/on courut
nous courions	nous courrons	nous courrions	
vous couriez	vous courrez	vous courriez	
ils/elles couraient	ils/elles courront	ils/elles courraient	ils/elles coururent

couvrir - to cover		for English tense meanings see pages 6 and 7
Impératif *Imperative*	*Présent* *Present*	*Passé composé* *Perfect*
	je couvre	j'ai couvert
couvre!	tu couvres	tu as couvert
	il couvre	il a couvert
	elle couvre	elle a couvert
	on couvre	on a couvert
couvrons!	nous couvrons	nous avons couvert
couvrez!	vous couvrez	vous avez couvert
	ils couvrent	ils ont couvert
	elles couvrent	elles ont couvert

Imparfait *Imperfect*	*Futur* *Future*	*Conditionnel* *Conditional*	*Passé simple* *Past Historic*
je couvrais	je couvrirai	je *couvrir*ais	
tu couvrais	tu couvriras	tu *couvrir*ais	
il/elle/on couvrait	il/elle/on couvrira	il/elle/on ---ait	il/elle/on couvrit
nous couvrions	nous couvrirons	nous ---ions	
vous couvriez	vous couvrirez	vous ---iez	
ils/elles couvraient	ils/elles couvriront	ils/elles ---aient	ils/elles couvrirent

craindre - to fear, to be afraid of   for English tense meanings see pages 6 and 7

Impératif *Imperative*	*Présent* *Present*	*Passé composé* *Perfect*	
	je crains	j'ai craint	
ne crains pas!	tu crains	tu as craint	
	il craint	il a craint	
	elle craint	elle a craint	
	on craint	on a craint	
ne craignons pas!	nous craignons	nous avons craint	
ne craignez pas!	vous craignez	vous avez craint	
	ils craignent	ils ont craint	
	elles craignent	elles ont craint	

Imparfait *Imperfect*	*Futur* *Future*	*Conditionnel* *Conditional*	*Passé simple* *Past Historic*
je craignais	je craindrai	je *craindr*ais	
tu craignais	tu craindras	tu *craindr*ais	
il/elle/on craignait	il/elle/on craindra	il/elle/on ---ait	il/elle/on craignit
nous craignions	nous craindrons	nous ---ions	
vous craigniez	vous craindrez	vous ---iez	
ils/elles craignaient	ils/elles craindront	ils/elles ---aient	ils/elles craignirent

croire - to believe, to think   for English tense meanings see pages 6 and 7

Impératif *Imperative*	*Présent* *Present*	*Passé composé* *Perfect*	
	je crois	j'ai cru	
crois!	tu crois	tu as cru	
	il croit	il a cru	
	elle croit	elle a cru	
	on croit	on a cru	
croyons!	nous croyons	nous avons cru	
croyez!	vous croyez	vous avez cru	
	ils croient	ils ont cru	
	elles croient	elles ont cru	

Imparfait *Imperfect*	*Futur* *Future*	*Conditionnel* *Conditional*	*Passé simple* *Past Historic*
je croyais	je croirai	je croirais	
tu croyais	tu croiras	tu croirais	
il/elle/on croyait	il/elle/on croira	il/elle/on croirait	il/elle/on crut
nous croyions	nous croirons	nous croirions	
vous croyiez	vous croirez	vous croiriez	
ils/elles croyaient	ils/elles croiront	ils/elles croiraient	ils/elles crurent

cueillir - to pick   NB **accueillir** and **recueillir** follow this pattern

Impératif *Imperative*	*Présent* *Present*	*Passé composé* *Perfect*	
	je cueille	j'ai cueilli	
cueille!	tu cueilles	tu as cueilli	
	il cueille	il a cueilli	
	elle cueille	elle a cueilli	
	on cueille	on a cueilli	
cueillons!	nous cueillons	nous avons cueilli	
cueillez!	vous cueillez	vous avez cueilli	
	ils cueillent	ils ont cueilli	
	elles cueillent	elles ont cueilli	

Imparfait *Imperfect*	*Futur* *Future*	*Conditionnel* *Conditional*	*Passé simple* *Past Historic*
je cueillais	je cueillerai	je *cueiller*ais	
tu cueillais	tu cueilleras	tu *cueiller*ais	
il/elle/on cueillait	il/elle/on cueillera	il/elle/on ---ait	il/elle/on cueillit
nous cueillions	nous cueillerons	nous ---ions	
vous cueilliez	vous cueillerez	vous ---iez	
ils cueillaient	ils/elles cueilleront	ils/elles ---aient	ils/elles cueillirent

découvrir - to discover   for English tense meanings see pages 6 and 7

Impératif *Imperative*	*Présent* *Present*	*Passé composé* *Perfect*	
	je découvre	j'ai découvert	
découvre!	tu découvres	tu as découvert	
	il découvre	il a découvert	
	elle découvre	elle a découvert	
	on découvre	on a découvert	
découvrons!	nous découvrons	nous avons découvert	
découvrez!	vous découvrez	vous avez découvert	
	ils découvrent	ils ont découvert	
	elles découvrent	elles ont découvert	

Imparfait *Imperfect*	*Futur* *Future*	*Conditionnel* *Conditional*	*Passé simple* *Past Historic*
je découvrais	je découvrirai	je *découvrir*ais	
tu découvrais	tu découvriras	tu *découvrir*ais	
il/elle/on découvrait	il/elle/on découvrira	il/elle/on ---ait	il/elle/on découvrit
nous découvrions	nous découvrirons	nous ---ions	
vous découvriez	vous découvrirez	vous ---iez	
ils/elles découvraient	ils/elles découvriront	ils/elles ---aient	ils/elles découvrirent

détruire - to destroy   for English tense meanings see pages 6 and 7

Impératif / Imperative	Présent / Present	Passé composé / Perfect
	je détruis	j'ai détruit
détruis!	tu détruis	tu as détruit
	il détruit	il a détruit
	elle détruit	elle a détruit
	on détruit	on a détruit
détruisons!	nous détruisons	nous avons détruit
détruisez!	vous détruisez	vous avez détruit
	ils détruisent	ils ont détruit
	elles détruisent	elles ont détruit

Imparfait / Imperfect	Futur / Future	Conditionnel / Conditional	Passé simple / Past Historic
je détruisais	je détruirai	je *détruir*ais	
tu détruisais	tu détruiras	tu *détruir*ais	
il/elle/on détruisait	il/elle/on détruira	il/elle/on ---ait	il/elle/on détruisit
nous détruisions	nous détruirons	nous ---ions	
vous détruisiez	vous détruirez	vous ---iez	
ils/elles détruisaient	ils/elles détruiront	ils/elles ---aient	ils/elles détruisirent

devenir* - to become   for English tense meanings see pages 6 and 7

Impératif / Imperative	Présent / Present	Passé composé / Perfect
	je deviens	je suis devenu(e)
deviens!	tu deviens	tu es devenu(e)
	il devient	il est devenu
	elle devient	elle est devenue
	on devient	on est devenu
devenons!	nous devenons	nous sommes devenu(e)s
devenez!	vous devenez	vous êtes devenu(e)(s)
	ils deviennent	ils sont devenus
	elles deviennent	elles sont devenues

Imparfait / Imperfect	Futur / Future	Conditionnel / Conditional	Passé simple / Past Historic
je devenais	je deviendrai	je *deviendr*ais	
tu devenais	tu deviendras	tu *deviendr*ais	
il/elle/on devenait	il/elle/on deviendra	il/elle/on ---ait	il/elle/on devint
nous devenions	nous deviendrons	nous ---ions	
vous deveniez	vous deviendrez	vous ---iez	
ils/elles devenaient	ils/elles deviendront	ils/elles ---aient	ils/elles devinrent

devoir - to have to   for English tense meanings see pages 6 and 7

Impératif Imperative	Présent Present	Passé composé Perfect
	je dois	j'ai dû
dois!	tu dois	tu as dû
	il doit	il a dû
	elle doit	elle a dû
	on doit	on a dû
devons!	nous devons	nous avons dû
devez!	vous devez	vous avez dû
	ils doivent	ils ont dû
	elles doivent	elles ont dû

Imparfait Imperfect	Futur Future	Conditionnel Conditional	Passé simple Past Historic
je devais	je devrai	je devrais	
tu devais	tu devras	tu devrais	
il/elle/on devait	il/elle/on devra	il/elle/on devrait	il/elle/on dut
nous devions	nous devrons	nous devrions	
vous deviez	vous devrez	vous devriez	
ils/elles devaient	ils/elles devront	ils/elles devraient	ils/elles durent

dire - to say, to tell   for English tense meanings see pages 6 and 7

Impératif Imperative	Présent Present	Passé composé Perfect
	je dis	j'ai dit
dis!	tu dis	tu as dit
	il dit	il a dit
	elle dit	elle a dit
	on dit	on a dit
disons!	nous disons	nous avons dit
dites!	vous dites	vous avez dit
	ils disent	ils ont dit
	elles disent	elles ont dit

Imparfait Imperfect	Futur Future	Conditionnel Conditional	Passé simple Past Historic
je disais	je dirai	je dirais	
tu disais	tu diras	tu dirais	
il/elle/on disait	il/elle/on dira	il/elle/on dirait	il/elle/on dit
nous disions	nous dirons	nous dirions	
vous disiez	vous direz	vous diriez	
ils/elles disaient	ils/elles diront	ils/elles diraient	ils/elles dirent

disparaître - to disappear   for English tense meanings see pages 6 and 7

Impératif Imperative	Présent Present	Passé composé Perfect	
	je disparais	j'ai disparu	
disparais!	tu disparais	tu as disparu	
	il disparaît	il a disparu	
	elle disparaît	elle a disparu	
	on disparaît	on a disparu	
disparaissons!	nous disparaissons	nous avons disparu	
disparaissez!	vous disparaissez	vous avez disparu	
	ils disparaissent	ils ont disparu	
	elles disparaissent	elles ont disparu	

Imparfait Imperfect	Futur Future	Conditionnel Conditional	Passé simple Past Historic
je disparaissais	je disparaîtrai	je *disparaître*ais	
tu disparaissais	tu disparaîtras	tu *disparaître*ais	
il/elle disparaissait	il/elle/on disparaîtra	il/elle/on ---ait	il/elle/on disparut
nous disparaissions	nous disparaîtrons	nous ---ions	
vous disparaissiez	vous disparaîtrez	vous ---iez	
ils disparaissaient	ils disparaîtront	ils ---aient	ils disparurent
elles disparaissaient	elles disparaîtront	elles ---aient	elles disparurent

dormir - to sleep   for English tense meanings see pages 6 and 7

Impératif Imperative	Présent Present	Passé composé Perfect	
	je dors	j'ai dormi	
dors!	tu dors	tu as dormi	
	il dort	il a dormi	
	elle dort	elle a dormi	
	on dort	on a dormi	
dormons!	nous dormons	nous avons dormi	
dormez!	vous dormez	vous avez dormi	
	ils dorment	ils ont dormi	
	elles dorment	elles ont dormi	

Imparfait Imperfect	Futur Future	Conditionnel Conditional	Passé simple Past Historic
je dormais	je dormirai	je *dormir*ais	
tu dormais	tu dormiras	tu *dormir*ais	
il/elle/on dormait	il/elle/on dormira	il/elle/on ---ait	il/elle/on dormit
nous dormions	nous dormirons	nous ---ions	
vous dormiez	vous dormirez	vous ---iez	
ils/elles dormaient	ils/elles dormiront	ils/elles ---aient	ils/elles dormirent

écrire - to write		for English tense meanings see pages 6 and 7
Impératif / *Imperative*	*Présent* / *Present*	*Passé composé* / *Perfect*
écris!	j'écris	j'ai écrit
	tu écris	tu as écrit
	il écrit	il a écrit
	elle écrit	elle a écrit
	on écrit	on a écrit
écrivons!	nous écrivons	nous avons écrit
écrivez!	vous écrivez	vous avez écrit
	ils écrivent	ils ont écrit
	elles écrivent	elles ont écrit

Imparfait / *Imperfect*	*Futur* / *Future*	*Conditionnel* / *Conditional*	*Passé simple* / *Past Historic*
j'écrivais	j'écrirai	j'écrirais	
tu écrivais	tu écriras	tu écrirais	
il/elle/on écrivait	il/elle/on écrira	il/elle/on écrirait	il/elle/on écrivit
nous écrivions	nous écrirons	nous écririons	
vous écriviez	vous écrirez	vous écririez	
ils/elles écrivaient	ils/elles écriront	ils/elles écriraient	ils/elles écrivirent

s'endormir* - to go to sleep, to fall asleep		for English tense meanings see pages 6 and 7
Impératif / *Imperative*	*Présent* / *Present*	*Passé composé* / *Perfect*
endors-toi!	je m'endors	je me suis endormi(e)
	tu t'endors	tu t'es endormi(e)
	il s'endort	il s'est endormi
	elle s'endort	elle s'est endormie
	on s'endort	on s'est endormi
endormons-nous!	nous nous endormons	nous nous sommes endormi(e)s
endormez-vous!	vous vous endormez	vous vous êtes endormi(e)(s)
	ils s'endorment	ils se sont endormis
	elles s'endorment	elles se sont endormies

Imparfait / *Imperfect*	*Futur* / *Future*	*Conditionnel* / *Conditional*	*Passé simple* / *Past Historic*
je m'endormais	je m'endormirai	je m'*endormir*ais	
tu t'endormais	tu t'endormiras	tu t'*endormir*ais	
il s'endormait	il/elle s'endormira	il/elle/on s'---ait	il/elle/on s'endormit
nous nous endormions	nous nous endormirons	nous nous ---ions	
vous vous endormiez	vous vous endormirez	vous vous ---iez	ils s'endormirent
ils/elles s'endormaient	ils/elles s'endormiront	ils/elles s'---aient	elles s'endormirent

entretenir - to maintain   for English tense meanings see pages 6 and 7

Impératif Imperative	Présent Present	Passé composé Perfect	
	j'entretiens	j'ai entretenu	
entretiens!	tu entretiens	tu as entretenu	
	il entretient	il a entretenu	
	elle entretient	elle a entretenu	
	on entretient	on a entretenu	
entretenons!	nous entretenons	nous avons entretenu	
entretenez!	vous entretenez	vous avez entretenu	
	ils entretiennent	ils ont entretenu	
	elles entretiennent	elles ont entretenu	

Imparfait Imperfect	Futur Future	Conditionnel Conditional	Passé simple Past Historic
j'entretenais	j'entretiendrai	j'*entretiendr*ais	
tu entretenais	tu entretiendras	tu *entretiendr*ais	
il/elle/on entretenait	il/elle entretiendra	il/elle ---ait	il/elle/on entretint
nous entretenions	nous entretiendrons	nous ---ions	
vous entreteniez	vous entretiendrez	vous ---iez	
ils/elles entretenaient	ils/elles entretiendront	ils/elles ---aient	ils/elles entretinrent

éteindre - to extinguish, to switch off   for English tense meanings see pages 6 and 7

Impératif Imperative	Présent Present	Passé composé Perfect	
	j'éteins	j'ai éteint	
éteins!	tu éteins	tu as éteint	
	il éteint	il a éteint	
	elle éteint	elle a éteint	
	on éteint	on a éteint	
éteignons!	nous éteignons	nous avons éteint	
éteignez!	vous éteignez	vous avez éteint	
	ils éteignent	ils ont éteint	
	elles éteignent	elles ont éteint	

Imparfait Imperfect	Futur Future	Conditionnel Conditional	Passé simple Past Historic
j'éteignais	j'éteindrai	j'*éteindr*ais	
tu éteignais	tu éteindras	tu *éteindr*ais	
il/elle/on éteignait	il/elle/on éteindra	il/elle/on ---ait	il/elle/on éteignit
nous éteignions	nous éteindrons	nous ---ions	
vous éteigniez	vous éteindrez	vous ---iez	
ils/elles éteignaient	ils/elles éteindront	ils/elles ---aient	ils/elles éteignirent

être - to be
for English tense meanings see pages 6 and 7

Impératif / *Imperative*	*Présent* / *Present*	*Passé composé* / *Perfect*
	je suis	j'ai été
sois!	tu es	tu as été
	il est	il a été
	elle est	elle a été
	on est	on a été
soyons!	nous sommes	nous avons été
soyez!	vous êtes	vous avez été
	ils sont	ils ont été
	elles sont	elles ont été

Imparfait / *Imperfect*	*Futur* / *Future*	*Conditionnel* / *Conditional*	*Passé simple* / *Past Historic*
j'étais	je serai	je serais	
tu étais	tu seras	tu serais	
il/elle/on était	il/elle/on sera	il/elle/on serait	il/elle/on fut
nous étions	nous serons	nous serions	
vous étiez	vous serez	vous seriez	
ils/elles étaient	ils/elles seront	ils/elles seraient	ils/elles furent

faire - to do, to make
for English tense meanings see pages 6 and 7

Impératif / *Imperative*	*Présent* / *Present*	*Passé composé* / *Perfect*
	je fais	j'ai fait
fais!	tu fais	tu as fait
	il fait	il a fait
	elle fait	elle a fait
	on fait	on a fait
faisons!	nous faisons	nous avons fait
faites!	vous faites	vous avez fait
	ils font	ils ont fait
	elles font	elles ont fait

Imparfait / *Imperfect*	*Futur* / *Future*	*Conditionnel* / *Conditional*	*Passé simple* / *Past Historic*
je faisais	je ferai	je ferais	
tu faisais	tu feras	tu ferais	
il/elle/on faisait	il/elle/on fera	il/elle/on ferait	il/elle/on fit
nous faisions	nous ferons	nous ferions	
vous faisiez	vous ferez	vous feriez	
ils/elles faisaient	ils/elles feront	ils/elles feraient	ils/elles firent

falloir - to have to		for English tense meanings see pages 6 and 7	
Impératif *Imperative*	*Présent* *Present*	*Passé composé* *Perfect*	
NONE	il faut	il a fallu	
Imparfait *Imperfect*	*Futur* *Future*	*Conditionnel* *Conditional*	*Passé simple* *Past Historic*
il fallait	il faudra	il faudrait	il fallut

Falloir only has an **il** form. It is sometimes called a defective verb.

lire - to read		for English tense meanings see pages 6 and 7	
Impératif *Imperative*	*Présent* *Present*	*Passé composé* *Perfect*	
	je lis	j'ai lu	
lis!	tu lis	tu as lu	
	il lit	il a lu	
	elle lit	elle a lu	
	on lit	on a lu	
lisons!	nous lisons	nous avons lu	
lisez!	vous lisez	vous avez lu	
	ils lisent	ils ont lu	
	elles lisent	elles ont lu	
Imparfait *Imperfect*	*Futur* *Future*	*Conditionnel* *Conditional*	*Passé simple* *Past Historic*
je lisais	je lirai	je lirais	
tu lisais	tu liras	tu lirais	
il/elle/on lisait	il/elle/on lira	il/elle/on lirait	il/elle/on lut
nous lisions	nous lirons	nous lirions	
vous lisiez	vous lirez	vous liriez	
ils/elles lisaient	ils/elles liront	ils/elles liraient	ils/elles lurent

mentir - to lie, to tell an untruth		for English tense meanings see pages 6 and 7	
Impératif **Imperative**	**Présent** **Present**	**Passé composé** **Perfect**	
	je mens	j'ai menti	
mens!	tu mens	tu as menti	
	il ment	il a menti	
	elle ment	elle a menti	
	on ment	on a menti	
mentons!	nous mentons	nous avons menti	
mentez!	vous mentez	vous avez menti	
	ils mentent	ils ont menti	
	elles mentent	elles ont menti	
Imparfait **Imperfect**	**Futur** **Future**	**Conditionnel** **Conditional**	**Passé simple** **Past Historic**
je mentais	je mentirai	je *mentir*ais	
tu mentais	tu mentiras	tu *mentir*ais	
il/elle/on mentait	il/elle/on mentira	il/elle/on ---ait	il/elle/on mentit
nous mentions	nous mentirons	nous ---ions	
vous mentiez	vous mentirez	vous ---iez	
ils/elles mentaient	ils/elles mentiront	ils/elles ---aient	ils/elles mentirent

mettre - to put		for English tense meanings see pages 6 and 7	
Impératif **Imperative**	**Présent** **Present**	**Passé composé** **Perfect**	
	je mets	j'ai mis	
mets!	tu mets	tu as mis	
	il met	il a mis	
	elle met	elle a mis	
	on met	on a mis	
mettons!	nous mettons	nous avons mis	
mettez!	vous mettez	vous avez mis	
	ils mettent	ils ont mis	
	elles mettent	elles ont mis	
Imparfait **Imperfect**	**Futur** **Future**	**Conditionnel** **Conditional**	**Passé simple** **Past Historic**
je mettais	je mettrai	je mettrais	
tu mettais	tu mettras	tu mettrais	
il/elle/on mettait	il/elle/on mettra	il/elle/on mettrait	il/elle/on mit
nous mettions	nous mettrons	nous mettrions	
vous mettiez	vous mettrez	vous mettriez	
ils/elles mettaient	ils/elles mettront	ils/elles mettraient	ils/elles mirent

se mettre* (à) - to start (to)   for English tense meanings see pages 6 and 7

Impératif / Imperative	Présent / Present	Passé composé / Perfect	
	je me mets	je me suis mis(e)	
mets-toi!	tu te mets	tu t'es mis(e)	
	il se met	il s'est mis	
	elle se met	elle s'est mise	
	on se met	on s'est mis	
mettons-nous!	nous nous mettons	nous nous sommes mis(es)	
mettez-vous!	vous vous mettez	vous vous êtes mis(e)/(es)	
	ils se mettent	ils se sont mis	
	elles se mettent	elles se sont mises	

Imparfait / Imperfect	Futur / Future	Conditionnel / Conditional	Passé simple / Past Historic
je me mettais	je me mettrai	je me *mettr*ais	
tu te mettais	tu te mettras	tu te *mettr*ais	
il/elle/on se mettait	il/elle/on se mettra	il/elle/on se ---ait	il/elle/on se mit
nous nous mettions	nous nous mettrons	nous nous ---ions	
vous vous mettiez	vous vous mettrez	vous vous ---iez	
ils/elles se mettaient	ils/elles se mettront	ils/elles se ---aient	ils/elles se mirent

mourir* - to die   for English tense meanings see pages 6 and 7

Impératif / Imperative	Présent / Present	Passé composé / Perfect	
	je meurs	je suis mort(e)	
meurs!	tu meurs	tu es mort(e)	
	il meurt	il est mort	
	elle meurt	elle est morte	
	on meurt	on est mort	
mourons!	nous mourons	nous sommes mort(e)s	
mourez!	vous mourez	vous êtes mort(e)(s)	
	ils meurent	ils sont morts	
	elles meurent	elles sont mortes	

Imparfait / Imperfect	Futur / Future	Conditionnel / Conditional	Passé simple / Past Historic
je mourais	je mourrai	je *mourr*ais	
tu mourais	tu mourras	tu *mourr*ais	
il/elle/on mourait	il/elle/on mourra	il/elle/on ---ait	il/elle/on mourut
nous mourions	nous mourrons	nous ---ions	
vous mouriez	vous mourrez	vous ---iez	
ils/elles mouraient	ils/elles mourront	ils/elles ---aient	ils/elles moururent

naître* - to be born
for English tense meanings see pages 6 and 7

Impératif / Imperative	Présent / Present	Passé composé / Perfect	
nais!	je nais	je suis né(e)	
	tu nais	tu es né(e)	
	il naît	il est né	
	elle naît	elle est née	
	on naît	on est né	
naissons!	nous naissons	nous sommes né(e)s	
naissez!	vous naissez	vous êtes né(e)(s)	
	ils naissent	ils sont nés	
	elles naissent	elles sont nées	

Imparfait / Imperfect	Futur / Future	Conditionnel / Conditional	Passé simple / Past Historic
je naissais	je naîtrai	je naîtrais	
tu naissais	tu naîtras	tu naîtrais	
il/elle/on naissait	il/elle/on naîtra	il/elle/on naîtrait	il/elle/on naquit
nous naissions	nous naîtrons	nous naîtrions	
vous naissiez	vous naîtrez	vous naîtriez	
ils/elles naissaient	ils/elles naîtront	ils/elles naîtraient	ils/elles naquirent

obtenir - to obtain
for English tense meanings see pages 6 and 7

Impératif / Imperative	Présent / Present	Passé composé / Perfect	
obtiens!	j'obtiens	j'ai obtenu	
	tu obtiens	tu as obtenu	
	il obtient	il a obtenu	
	elle obtient	elle a obtenu	
	on obtient	on a obtenu	
obtenons!	nous obtenons	nous avons obtenu	
obtenez!	vous obtenez	vous avez obtenu	
	ils obtiennent	ils ont obtenu	
	elles obtiennent	elles ont obtenu	

Imparfait / Imperfect	Futur / Future	Conditionnel / Conditional	Passé simple / Past Historic
j'obtenais	j'obtiendrai	j'obtiendrais	
tu obtenais	tu obtiendras	tu obtiendrais	
il/elle/on obtenait	il/elle/on obtiendra	il/elle/on ---ait	il/elle/on obtint
nous obtenions	nous obtiendrons	nous ---ions	
vous obteniez	vous obtiendrez	vous ---iez	
ils/elles obtenaient	ils/elles obtiendront	ils/elles ---aient	ils/elles obtinrent

offrir - to offer		for English tense meanings see pages 6 and 7

Impératif Imperative	Présent Present	Passé composé Perfect
	j'offre	j'ai offert
offre!	tu offres	tu as offert
	il offre	il a offert
	elle offre	elle a offert
	on offre	on a offert
offrons!	nous offrons	nous avons offert
offrez!	vous offrez	vous avez offert
	ils offrent	ils ont offert
	elles offrent	elles ont offert

Imparfait Imperfect	Futur Future	Conditionnel Conditional	Passé simple Past Historic
j'offrais	j'offrirai	j'offrirais	
tu offrais	tu offriras	tu offrirais	
il/elle/on offrait	il/elle/on offrira	il/elle/on offrirait	il/elle/on offrit
nous offrions	nous offrirons	nous offririons	
vous offriez	vous offrirez	vous offririez	
ils/elles offraient	ils/elles offriront	ils/elles offriraient	ils/elles offrirent

ouvrir - to open		for English tense meanings see pages 6 and 7

Impératif Imperative	Présent Present	Passé composé Perfect
	j'ouvre	j'ai ouvert
ouvre!	tu ouvres	tu as ouvert
	il ouvre	il a ouvert
	elle ouvre	elle a ouvert
	on ouvre	on a ouvert
ouvrons!	nous ouvrons	nous avons ouvert
ouvrez!	vous ouvrez	vous avez ouvert
	ils ouvrent	ils ont ouvert
	elles ouvrent	elles ont ouvert

Imparfait Imperfect	Futur Future	Conditionnel Conditional	Passé simple Past Historic
j'ouvrais	j'ouvrirai	j'*ouvrir*ais	
tu ouvrais	tu ouvriras	tu *ouvrir*ais	
il/elle/on ouvrait	il/elle/on ouvrira	il/elle/on ---ait	il/elle/on ouvrit
nous ouvrions	nous ouvrirons	nous ---ions	
vous ouvriez	vous ouvrirez	vous ---iez	
ils/elles ouvraient	ils/elles ouvriront	ils/elles ---aient	ils/elles ouvrirent

paraître - to appear, to seem   for English tense meanings see pages 6 and 7

Impératif Imperative	Présent Present	Passé composé Perfect	
	je parais	j'ai paru	
parais!	tu parais	tu as paru	
	il paraît	il a paru	
	elle paraît	elle a paru	
	on paraît	on a paru	
paraissons!	nous paraissons	nous avons paru	
paraissez!	vous paraissez	vous avez paru	
	ils paraissent	ils ont paru	
	elles paraissent	elles ont paru	

Imparfait Imperfect	Futur Future	Conditionnel Conditional	Passé simple Past Historic
je paraissais	je paraîtrai	je *paraîtr*ais	
tu paraissais	tu paraîtras	tu *paraîtr*ais	
il/elle/on paraissait	il/elle/on paraîtra	il/elle/on ---ait	il/elle/on parut
nous paraissions	nous paraîtrons	nous ---ions	
vous paraissiez	vous paraîtrez	vous ---iez	
ils/elles paraissaient	ils/elles paraîtront	ils/elles ---aient	ils/elles parurent

partir* - to leave   for English tense meanings see pages 6 and 7

Impératif Imperative	Présent Present	Passé composé Perfect	
	je pars	je suis parti(e)	
pars!	tu pars	tu es parti(e)	
	il part	il est parti	
	elle part	elle est partie	
	on part	on est parti	
partons!	nous partons	nous sommes parti(e)s	
partez!	vous partez	vous êtes parti(e)(s)	
	ils partent	ils sont partis	
	elles partent	elles sont parties	

Imparfait Imperfect	Futur Future	Conditionnel Conditional	Passé simple Past Historic
je partais	je partirai	je partirais	
tu partais	tu partiras	tu partirais	
il/elle/on partait	il/elle/on partira	il/elle/on partirait	il/elle/on partit
nous partions	nous partirons	nous partirions	
vous partiez	vous partirez	vous partiriez	
ils/elles partaient	ils/elles partiront	ils/elles partiraient	ils/elles partirent

peindre - to paint		for English tense meanings see pages 6 and 7
Impératif / *Imperative*	**Présent** / *Present*	**Passé composé** / *Perfect*
	je peins	j'ai peint
peins!	tu peins	tu as peint
	il peint	il a peint
	elle peint	elle a peint
	on peint	on a peint
peignons!	nous peignons	nous avons peint
peignez!	vous peignez	vous avez peint
	ils peignent	ils ont peint
	elles peignent	elles ont peint

Imparfait / *Imperfect*	**Futur** / *Future*	**Conditionnel** / *Conditional*	**Passé simple** / *Past Historic*
je peignais	je peindrai	je *peindr*ais	
tu peignais	tu peindras	tu *peindr*ais	
il/elle/on peignait	il/elle/on peindra	il/elle/on ---ait	il/elle/on peigna
nous peignions	nous peindrons	nous ---ions	
vous peigniez	vous peindrez	vous ---iez	
ils/elles peignaient	ils/elles peindront	ils/elles ---aient	ils/elles peignèrent

permettre - to allow		for English tense meanings see pages 6 and 7
Impératif / *Imperative*	**Présent** / *Present*	**Passé composé** / *Perfect*
	je permets	j'ai permis
permets!	tu permets	tu as permis
	il permet	il a permis
	elle permet	elle a permis
	on permet	on a permis
permettons!	nous permettons	nous avons permis
permettez!	vous permettez	vous avez permis
	ils permettent	ils ont permis
	elles permettent	elles ont permis

Imparfait / *Imperfect*	**Futur** / *Future*	**Conditionnel** / *Conditional*	**Passé simple** / *Past Historic*
je permettais	je permettrai	je *permettr*ais	
tu permettais	tu permettras	tu *permettr*ais	
il/elle/on permettait	il/elle/on permettra	il/elle/on ---ait	il/elle/on permit
nous permettions	nous permettrons	nous ---ions	
vous permettiez	vous permettrez	vous ---iez	
ils/elles permettaient	ils/elles permettront	ils/elles ---aient	ils/elles permirent

pleuvoir - to rain		for English tense meanings see pages 6 and 7	
Impératif *Imperative*	*Présent* *Present*	*Passé composé* *Perfect*	
NONE	il pleut	il a plu	
Imparfait *Imperfect*	*Futur* *Future*	*Conditionnel* *Conditional*	*Passé simple* *Past Historic*
il pleuvait	il pleuvra	il pleuvrait	il plut

Pleuvoir only has an **il** form. It is sometimes called a defective verb.

pouvoir - to be able to		for English tense meanings see pages 6 and 7	
Impératif *Imperative*	*Présent* *Present*	*Passé composé* *Perfect*	
NONE	je peux (puis-je?) tu peux il peut elle peut on peut nous pouvons vous pouvez ils peuvent elles peuvent	j'ai pu tu as pu il a pu elle a pu on a pu nous avons pu vous avez pu ils ont pu elles ont pu	
Imparfait *Imperfect*	*Futur* *Future*	*Conditionnel* *Conditional*	*Passé simple* *Past Historic*
je pouvais tu pouvais il/elle/on pouvait nous pouvions vous pouviez ils/elles pouvaient	je pourrai tu pourras il/elle/on pourra nous pourrons vous pourrez ils/elles pourront	je pourrais tu pourrais il/elle/on pourrait nous pourrions vous pourriez ils/elles pourraient	 il/elle/on put ils/elles purent

prendre - to take		for English tense meanings see pages 6 and 7
Impératif *Imperative*	*Présent* *Present*	*Passé composé* *Perfect*
prends!	je prends	j'ai pris
	tu prends	tu as pris
	il prend	il a pris
	elle prend	elle a pris
	on prend	on a pris
prenons!	nous prenons	nous avons pris
prenez!	vous prenez	vous avez pris
	ils prennent	ils ont pris
	elles prennent	elles ont pris

Imparfait *Imperfect*	*Futur* *Future*	*Conditionnel* *Conditional*	*Passé simple* *Past Historic*
je prenais	je prendrai	je *prendr*ais	
tu prenais	tu prendras	tu *prendr*ais	
il/elle/on prenait	il/elle/on prendra	il/elle/on ---ait	il/elle/on prit
nous prenions	nous prendrons	nous ---ions	
vous preniez	vous prendrez	vous ---iez	
ils/elles prenaient	ils/elles prendront	ils/elles ---aient	ils/elle prirent

prévenir - to warn, to inform		for English tense meanings see pages 6 and 7
Impératif *Imperative*	*Présent* *Present*	*Passé composé* *Perfect*
préviens!	je préviens	j'**ai** prévenu
	tu préviens	tu **as** prévenu
	il prévient	il **a** prévenu
	elle prévient	elle **a** prévenu
	on prévient	on **a** prévenu
prévenons!	nous prévenons	nous **avons** prévenu
prévenez!	vous prévenez	vous **avez** prévenu
	ils préviennent	ils **ont** prévenu
	elles préviennent	elles **ont** prévenu

Imparfait *Imperfect*	*Futur* *Future*	*Conditionnel* *Conditional*	*Passé simple* *Past Historic*
je prévenais	je préviendrai	je *préviendr*ais	
tu prévenais	tu préviendras	tu *préviendr*ais	
il/elle/on prévenait	il/elle/on préviendra	il/elle/on ---ait	il/elle/on prévint
nous prévenions	nous préviendrons	nous ---ions	
vous préveniez	vous préviendrez	vous ---iez	
ils/elles prévenaient	ils/elles préviendront	ils/elles ---aient	ils/elles prévinrent

recevoir - to receive   for English tense meanings see pages 6 and 7

Impératif Imperative	Présent Present	Passé composé Perfect	
	je reçois	j'ai reçu	
reçois!	tu reçois	tu as reçu	
	il reçoit	il a reçu	
	elle reçoit	elle a reçu	
	on reçoit	on a reçu	
recevons!	nous recevons	nous avons reçu	
recevez!	vous recevez	vous avez reçu	
	ils reçoivent	ils ont reçu	
	elles reçoivent	elles ont reçu	

Imparfait Imperfect	Futur Future	Conditionnel Conditional	Passé simple Past Historic
je recevais	je recevrai	je *recevr*ais	
tu recevais	tu recevras	tu *recevr*ais	
il/elle/on recevait	il/elle/on recevra	il/elle/on ---ait	il/elle/on reçut
nous recevions	nous recevrons	nous ---ions	
vous receviez	vous recevrez	vous ---iez	
ils/elles recevaient	ils/elles recevront	ils/elles ---aient	ils/elles reçurent

reconnaître - to recognise   for English tense meanings see pages 6 and 7

Impératif Imperative	Présent Present	Passé composé Perfect	
	je reconnais	j'ai reconnu	
reconnais!	tu reconnais	tu as reconnu	
	il reconnaît	il a reconnu	
	elle reconnaît	elle a reconnu	
	on reconnaît	on a reconnu	
reconnaissons!	nous reconnaissons	nous avons reconnu	
reconnaissez!	vous reconnaissez	vous avez reconnu	
	ils reconnaissent	ils ont reconnu	
	elles reconnaissent	elles ont reconnu	

Imparfait Imperfect	Futur Future	Conditionnel Conditional	Passé simple Past Historic
je reconnaissais	je reconnaîtrai	je *reconnaîtr*ais	
tu reconnaissais	tu reconnaîtras	tu *reconnaîtr*ais	
il/elle/on reconnaissait	il/elle/on reconnaîtra	il/elle/on ---ait	il/elle/on reconnut
nous reconnaissions	nous reconnaîtrons	nous ---ions	
vous reconnaissiez	vous reconnaîtrez	vous ---iez	
ils reconnaissaient	ils reconnaîtront	ils ---aient	ils reconnurent
elles reconnaissaient	elles reconnaîtront	elles ---aient	elles reconnurent

repartir* - to leave again		for English tense meanings see pages 6 and 7
Impératif / **Imperative**	**Présent** / **Present**	**Passé composé** / **Perfect**
	je repars	je suis reparti(e)
repars!	tu repars	tu es reparti(e)
	il repart	il est reparti
	elle repart	elle est repartie
	on repart	on est reparti
repartons!	nous repartons	nous sommes reparti(e)s
repartez!	vous repartez	vous êtes reparti(e)(s)
	ils repartent	ils sont repartis
	elles repartent	elles sont reparties

Imparfait / **Imperfect**	**Futur** / **Future**	**Conditionnel** / **Conditional**	**Passé simple** / **Past Historic**
je repartais	je repartirai	je *repartir*ais	
tu repartais	tu repartiras	tu *repartir*ais	
il/elle/on repartait	il/elle/on repartira	il/elle/on ---ait	il/elle/on repartit
nous repartions	nous repartirons	nous ---ions	
vous repartiez	vous repartirez	vous ---iez	
ils/elles repartaient	ils/elles repartiront	ils/elles ---aient	ils/elles repartirent

reprendre - to take back, to resume		for English tense meanings see pages 6 and 7
Impératif / **Imperative**	**Présent** / **Present**	**Passé composé** / **Perfect**
	je reprends	j'ai repris
reprends!	tu reprends	tu as repris
	il reprend	il a repris
	elle reprend	elle a repris
	on reprend	on a repris
reprenons!	nous reprenons	nous avons repris
reprenez!	vous reprenez	vous avez repris
	ils reprennent	ils ont repris
	elles reprennent	elles ont repris

Imparfait / **Imperfect**	**Futur** / **Future**	**Conditionnel** / **Conditional**	**Passé simple** / **Past Historic**
je reprenais	je reprendrai	je *reprendr*ais	
tu reprenais	tu reprendras	tu *reprendr*ais	
il/elle/on reprenait	il/elle/on reprendra	il/elle/on ---ait	il/elle/on reprit
nous reprenions	nous reprendrons	nous ---ions	
vous repreniez	vous reprendrez	vous ---iez	
ils/elles reprenaient	ils/elles reprendront	ils/elles ---aient	ils/elles reprirent

retenir - to hold back, to keep   for English tense meanings see pages 6 and 7

Impératif Imperative	Présent Present	Passé composé Perfect	
	je retiens	j'ai retenu	
retiens!	tu retiens	tu as retenu	
	il retient	il a retenu	
	elle retient	elle a retenu	
	on retient	on a retenu	
retenons!	nous retenons	nous avons retenu	
retenez!	vous retenez	vous avez retenu	
	ils retiennent	ils ont retenu	
	elles retiennent	elles ont retenu	

Imparfait Imperfect	Futur Future	Conditionnel Conditional	Passé simple Past Historic
je retenais	je retiendrai	je *retiendr*ais	
tu retenais	tu retiendras	tu *retiendr*ais	
il/elle/on retenait	il/elle/on retiendra	il/elle/on ---ait	il/elle/on retint
nous retenions	nous retiendrons	nous ---ions	
vous reteniez	vous retiendrez	vous ---iez	
ils/elles retenaient	ils/elles retiendront	ils/elles ---aient	ils/elles retinrent

revenir* - to come back, to return   for English tense meanings see pages 6 and 7

Impératif Imperative	Présent Present	Passé composé Perfect	
	je reviens	je suis revenu(e)	
reviens!	tu reviens	tu es revenu(e)	
	il revient	il est revenu	
	elle revient	elle est revenue	
	on revient	on est revenu	
revenons!	nous revenons	nous sommes revenu(e)s	
revenez!	vous revenez	vous êtes revenu(e)(s)	
	ils reviennent	ils sont revenus	
	elles reviennent	elles sont revenues	

Imparfait Imperfect	Futur Future	Conditionnel Conditional	Passé simple Past Historic
je revenais	je reviendrai	je *reviendr*ais	
tu revenais	tu reviendras	tu *reviendr*ais	
il/elle/on revenait	il/elle/on reviendra	il/elle/on ---ait	il/elle/on revint
nous revenions	nous reviendrons	nous ---ions	
voue reveniez	vous reviendrez	vous ---iez	
ils/elles revenaient	ils/elles reviendront	ils/elles ---aient	ils/elles revinrent

rire - to laugh   for English tense meanings see pages 6 and 7

Impératif Imperative	Présent Present	Passé composé Perfect	
	je ris	j'ai ri	
ris!	tu ris	tu as ri	
	il rit	il a ri	
	elle rit	elle a ri	
	on rit	on a ri	
rions!	nous rions	nous avons ri	
riez!	vous riez	vous avez ri	
	ils rient	ils ont ri	
	elles rient	elles ont ri	

Imparfait Imperfect	Futur Future	Conditionnel Conditional	Passé simple Past Historic
je riais	je rirai	je rirais	
tu riais	tu riras	tu rirais	
il/elle/on riait	il/elle/on rira	il/elle/on rirait	il/elle/on rit
nous riions	nous rirons	nous ririons	
vous riiez	vous rirez	vous ririez	
ils/elles riaient	ils/elles riront	ils/elles riraient	ils/elles rirent

savoir - to know (a fact, how to do sthg)   for English tense meanings see pages 6 and 7

Impératif Imperative	Présent Present	Passé composé Perfect	
	je sais	j'ai su	
sache!	tu sais	tu as su	
	il sait	il a su	
	elle sait	elle a su	
	on sait	on a su	
sachons!	nous savons	nous avons su	
sachez!	vous savez	vous avez su	
	ils savent	ils ont su	
	elles savent	elles ont su	

Imparfait Imperfect	Futur Future	Conditionnel Conditional	Passé simple Past Historic
je savais	je saurai	je saurais	
tu savais	tu sauras	tu saurais	
il/elle/on savait	il/elle/on saura	il/elle/on saurait	il/elle/on sut
nous savions	nous saurons	nous saurions	
vous saviez	vous saurez	vous sauriez	
ils/elles savaient	ils/elles sauront	ils/elles sauraient	ils/elles surent

sentir - to smell   for English tense meanings see pages 6 and 7

Impératif Imperative	Présent Present	Passé composé Perfect	
	je sens	j'ai senti	
sens!	tu sens	tu as senti	
	il sent	il a senti	
	elle sent	elle a senti	
	on sent	on a senti	
sentons!	nous sentons	nous avons senti	
sentez!	vous sentez	vous avez senti	
	ils sentent	ils ont senti	
	elles sentent	elles ont senti	

Imparfait Imperfect	Futur Future	Conditionnel Conditional	Passé simple Past Historic
je sentais	je sentirai	je sentirais	
tu sentais	tu sentiras	tu sentirais	
il/elle/on sentait	il/elle/on sentira	il/elle/on sentirait	il/elle/on sentit
nous sentions	nous sentirons	nous sentirions	
vous sentiez	vous sentirez	vous sentiriez	
ils/elles sentaient	ils/elles sentiront	ils/elles sentiraient	ils/elles sentirent

se sentir* - to feel (ill, well etc)   for English tense meanings see pages 6 and 7

Impératif Imperative	Présent Present	Passé composé Perfect	
	je me sens	je me suis senti(e)	
sens-toi!	tu te sens	tu t'es senti(e)	
	il se sent	il s'est senti	
	elle se sent	elle s'est sentie	
	on se sent	on s'est senti	
sentons-nous!	nous nous sentons	nous nous sommes senti(e)s	
sentez-vous!	vous vous sentez	vous vous êtes senti(e)(s)	
	ils se sentent	ils se sont sentis	
	elles se sentent	elles se sont senties	

Imparfait Imperfect	Futur Future	Conditionnel Conditional	Passé simple Past Historic
je me sentais	je me sentirai	je me *sentir*ais	
tu te sentais	tu te sentiras	tu te *sentir*ais	
il/elle/on se sentait	il/elle/on se sentira	il/elle/on se ---ait	il/elle/on se sentit
nous nous sentions	nous nous sentirons	nous nous ---ions	
vous vous sentiez	vous vous sentirez	vous vous ---iez	
ils/elles se sentaient	ils/elles se sentiront	ils/elles se ---aient	ils/elles se sentirent

servir - to serve   for English tense meanings see pages 6 and 7

Impératif Imperative	Présent Present	Passé composé Perfect	
	je sers	j'ai servi	
sers!	tu sers	tu as servi	
	il sert	il a servi	
	elle sert	elle a servi	
	on sert	on a servi	
servons!	nous servons	nous avons servi	
servez!	vous servez	vous avez servi	
	ils servent	ils ont servi	
	elles servent	elles ont servi	

Imparfait Imperfect	Futur Future	Conditionnel Conditional	Passé simple Past Historic
je servais	je servirai	je servirais	
tu servais	tu serviras	tu servirais	
il/elle/on servait	il/elle/on servira	il/elle/on servirait	il/elle/on servit
nous servions	nous servirons	nous servirions	
vous serviez	vous servirez	vous serviriez	
ils/elles servaient	ils/elles serviront	ils/elles serviraient	ils/elles servirent

se servir* - to help oneself, (+ **de**) to use   for English tense meanings see 6 and 7

Impératif Imperative	Présent Present	Passé composé Perfect	
	je me sers	je me suis servi(e)	
sers-toi!	tu te sers	tu t'es servi(e)	
	il se sert	il s'est servi	
	elle se sert	elle s'est servie	
	on se sert	on s'est servi	
servons-nous!	nous nous servons	nous nous sommes servi(e)s	
servez-vous!	vous vous servez	vous vous êtes servi(e)(s)	
	ils se servent	ils se sont servis	
	elles se servent	elles se sont servies	

Imparfait Imperfect	Futur Future	Conditionnel Conditional	Passé simple Past Historic
je me servais	je me servirai	je me *servir*ais	
tu te servais	tu te serviras	tu te *servir*ais	
il/elle/on se servait	il/elle/on se servira	il/elle/on se ---ait	il/elle/on se servit
nous nous servions	nous nous servirons	nous nous ---ions	
vous vous serviez	vous vous servirez	vous vous ---iez	
ils/elles se servaient	ils/elles se serviront	ils/elles se ---aient	ils/elles se servirent

sortir* - to go out		for English tense meanings see pages 6 and 7
Impératif / *Imperative*	**Présent** / *Present*	**Passé composé** / *Perfect*
	je sors	je suis sorti(e)
sors!	tu sors	tu es sorti(e)
	il sort	il est sorti
	elle sort	elle est sortie
	on sort	on est sorti
sortons!	nous sortons	nous sommes sorti(e)s
sortez!	vous sortez	vous êtes sorti(e)(s)
	ils sortent	ils sont sortis
	elles sortent	elles sont sorties

Imparfait / *Imperfect*	**Futur** / *Future*	**Conditionnel** / *Conditional*	**Passé simple** / *Past Historic*
je sortais	je sortirai	je sortirais	
tu sortais	tu sortiras	tu sortirais	
il/elle/on sortait	il/elle/on sortira	il/elle/on sortirait	il/elle/on sortit
nous sortions	nous sortirons	nous sortirions	
vous sortiez	vous sortirez	vous sortiriez	
ils/elles sortaient	ils/elles sortiront	ils/elles sortiraient	ils/elles sortirent

souffrir - to suffer		for English tense meanings see pages 6 and 7
Impératif / *Imperative*	**Présent** / *Present*	**Passé composé** / *Perfect*
	je souffre	j'ai souffert
souffre!	tu souffres	tu as souffert
	il souffre	il a souffert
	elle souffre	elle a souffert
	on souffre	on a souffert
souffrons!	nous souffrons	nous avons souffert
souffrez!	vous souffrez	vous avez souffert
	ils souffrent	ils ont souffert
	elles souffrent	elles ont souffert

Imparfait / *Imperfect*	**Futur** / *Future*	**Conditionnel** / *Conditional*	**Passé simple** / *Past Historic*
je souffrais	je souffrirai	je *souffrir*ais	
tu souffrais	tu souffriras	tu *souffrir*ais	
il/elle/on souffrait	il/elle/on souffrira	il/elle/on ---ait	il/elle/on souffrit
nous souffrions	nous souffrirons	nous ---ions	
vous souffriez	vous souffrirez	vous ---iez	
ils/elles souffraient	ils/elles souffriront	ils/elles ---aient	ils/elles souffrirent

sourire - to smile   for English tense meanings see pages 6 and 7

Impératif / Imperative	Présent / Present	Passé composé / Perfect	
souris!	je souris	j'ai souri	
	tu souris	tu as souri	
	il sourit	il a souri	
	elle sourit	elle a souri	
	on sourit	on a souri	
sourions!	nous sourions	nous avons souri	
souriez!	vous souriez	vous avez souri	
	ils sourient	ils ont souri	
	elles sourient	elles ont souri	

Imparfait / Imperfect	Futur / Future	Conditionnel / Conditional	Passé simple / Past Historic
je souriais	je sourirai	je *sourir*ais	
tu souriais	tu souriras	tu *sourir*ais	
il/elle/on souriait	il/elle/on sourira	il/elle/on ---ait	il/elle/on sourit
nous souriions	nous sourirons	nous ---ions	
vous souriiez	vous sourirez	vous ---iez	
ils/elles souriaient	ils/elles souriront	ils/elles ---aient	ils/elles sourirent

se souvenir* (de) - to remember   for English tense meanings see pages 6 and 7

Impératif / Imperative	Présent / Present	Passé composé / Perfect	
souviens-toi!	je me souviens	je me suis souvenu(e)	
	tu te souviens	tu t'es souvenu(e)	
	il se souvient	il s'est souvenu	
	elle se souvient	elle s'est souvenue	
	on se souvient	on s'est souvenu	
souvenons-nous!	nous nous souvenons	nous nous sommes souvenu(e)s	
souvenez-vous!	vous vous souvenez	vous vous êtes souvenu(e)(s)	
	ils se souviennent	ils se sont souvenus	
	elles se souviennent	elles se sont souvenues	

Imparfait / Imperfect	Futur / Future	Conditionnel / Conditional	Passé simple / Past Historic
je me souvenais	je me souviendrai	je me *souviendr*ais	
tu te souvenais	tu te souviendras	tu te *souviendr*ais	
il/elle/on se souvenait	il/elle se souviendra	il/elle/on se ---ait	il/elle/on se souvint
nous nous souvenions	nous nous souviendrons	nous nous ---ions	
		vous vous ---iez	
vous vous souveniez	vous vous souviendrez	ils/elles se ---aient	ils/elles se souvinrent
ils/elles se souvenaient	ils se souviendront		

suivre - to follow		for English tense meanings see pages 6 and 7
Impératif *Imperative*	**Présent** *Present*	**Passé composé** *Perfect*
	je suis	j'ai suivi
suis!	tu suis	tu as suivi
	il suit	il a suivi
	elle suit	elle a suivi
	on suit	on a suivi
suivons!	nous suivons	nous avons suivi
suivez!	vous suivez	vous avez suivi
	ils suivent	ils ont suivi
	elles suivent	elles ont suivi

Imparfait *Imperfect*	**Futur** *Future*	**Conditionnel** *Conditional*	**Passé simple** *Past Historic*
je suivais	je suivrai	je suivrais	
tu suivais	tu suivras	tu suivrais	
il/elle/on suivait	il/elle/on suivra	il/elle/on suivrait	il/elle/on suivit
nous suivions	nous suivrons	nous suivrions	
vous suiviez	vous suivrez	vous suivriez	
ils/elles suivaient	ils/elles suivront	ils/elles suivraient	ils/elles suivirent

surprendre - to surprise		for English tense meanings see pages 6 and 7
Impératif *Imperative*	**Présent** *Present*	**Passé composé** *Perfect*
	je surprends	j'ai surpris
surprends!	tu surprends	tu as surpris
	il surprend	il a surpris
	elle surprend	elle a surpris
	on surprend	on a surpris
surprenons!	nous surprenons	nous avons surpris
surprenez!	vous surprenez	vous avez surpris
	ils surprennent	ils ont surpris
	elles surprennent	elles ont surpris

Imparfait *Imperfect*	**Futur** *Future*	**Conditionnel** *Conditional*	**Passé simple** *Past Historic*
je surprenais	je surprendrai	je *surprendr*ais	
tu surprenais	tu surprendras	tu *surprendr*ais	
il/elle/on surprenait	il/elle/on surprendra	il/elle/on ---ait	il/elle/on surprit
nous surprenions	nous surprendrons	nous ---ions	
vous surpreniez	vous surprendrez	vous ---iez	
ils/elles surprenaient	ils/elles surprendront	ils/elles ---aient	ils/elles surprirent

tenir - to hold, to keep		for English tense meanings see pages 6 and 7
Impératif / **Imperative**	**Présent** / **Present**	**Passé composé** / **Perfect**
	je tiens	j'ai tenu
tiens!	tu tiens	tu as tenu
	il tient	il a tenu
	elle tient	elle a tenu
	on tient	on a tenu
tenons!	nous tenons	nous avons tenu
tenez!	vous tenez	vous avez tenu
	ils tiennent	ils ont tenu
	elles tiennent	elles ont tenu

Imparfait / **Imperfect**	**Futur** / **Future**	**Conditionnel** / **Conditional**	**Passé simple** / **Past Historic**
je tenais	je tiendrai	je *tiendr*ais	
tu tenais	tu tiendras	tu *tiendr*ais	
il/elle/on tenait	il/elle/on tiendra	il/elle/on ---ait	il/elle/on tint
nous tenions	nous tiendrons	nous ---ions	
vous teniez	vous tiendrez	vous ---iez	
ils/elles tenaient	ils/elles tiendront	ils/elles ---aient	ils/elles tinrent

se tenir* - to stand		for English tense meanings see pages 6 and 7
Impératif / **Imperative**	**Présent** / **Present**	**Passé composé** / **Perfect**
	je me tiens	je me suis tenu(e)
tiens-toi!	tu te tiens	tu t'es tenu(e)
	il se tient	il s'est tenu
	elle se tient	elle s'est tenue
	on se tient	on s'est tenu
tenons-nous!	nous nous tenons	nous nous sommes tenu(e)s
tenez-vous!	vous vous tenez	vous vous êtes tenu(e)(s)
	ils se tiennent	ils se sont tenus
	elles se tiennent	elles se sont tenues

Imparfait / **Imperfect**	**Futur** / **Future**	**Conditionnel** / **Conditional**	**Passé simple** / **Past Historic**
je me tenais	je me tiendrai	je me *tiendr*ais	
tu te tenais	tu te tiendras	tu te *tiendr*ais	
il/elle/on se tenait	il/elle/on se tiendra	il/elle/on se ---ait	il/elle/on se tint
nous nous tenions	nous nous tiendrons	nous nous ---ions	
vous vous teniez	vous vous tiendrez	vous vous ---iez	
ils/elles se tenaient	ils/elles se tiendront	ils/elles se ---aient	ils/elles se tinrent

venir* - to come		for English tense meanings see pages 6 and 7	
Impératif / *Imperative*	**Présent** / *Present*	**Passé composé** / *Perfect*	
	je viens	je suis venu(e)	
viens!	tu viens	tu es venu(e)	
	il vient	il est venu	
	elle vient	elle est venue	
	on vient	on est venu	
venons!	nous venons	nous sommes venu(e)s	
venez!	vous venez	vous êtes venu(e)(s)	
	ils viennent	ils sont venus	
	elles viennent	elles sont venues	
Imparfait / *Imperfect*	**Futur** / *Future*	**Conditionnel** / *Conditional*	**Passé simple** / *Past Historic*
je venais	je viendrai	je *viendr*ais	
tu venais	tu viendras	tu *viendr*ais	
il/elle/on venait	il/elle/on viendra	il/elle/on ---ait	il/elle/on vint
nous venions	nous viendrons	nous ---ions	
vous veniez	vous viendrez	vous ---iez	
ils/elles venaient	ils/elles viendront	ils/elles ---aient	ils/elles vinrent

vivre - to live, to be alive		for English tense meanings see pages 6 and 7	
Impératif / *Imperative*	**Présent** / *Present*	**Passé composé** / *Perfect*	
	je vis	j'ai vécu	
vis!	tu vis	tu as vécu	
	il vit	il a vécu	
	elle vit	elle a vécu	
	on vit	on a vécu	
vivons!	nous vivons	nous avons vécu	
vivez!	vous vivez	vous avez vécu	
	ils vivent	ils ont vécu	
	elles vivent	elles ont vécu	
Imparfait / *Imperfect*	**Futur** / *Future*	**Conditionnel** / *Conditional*	**Passé simple** / *Past Historic*
je vivais	je vivrai	je vivrais	
tu vivais	tu vivras	tu vivrais	
il/elle/on vivait	il/elle/on vivra	il/elle/on vivrait	il/elle/on vécut
nous vivions	nous vivrons	nous vivrions	
vous viviez	vous vivrez	vous vivriez	
ils/elles vivaient	ils/elles vivront	ils/elles vivraient	ils/elles vécurent

voir - to see   for English tense meanings see pages 6 and 7

Impératif Imperative	Présent Present	Passé composé Perfect	
	je vois	j'ai vu	
vois!	tu vois	tu as vu	
	il voit	il a vu	
	elle voit	elle a vu	
	on voit	on a vu	
voyons!	nous voyons	nous avons vu	
voyez!	vous voyez	vous avez vu	
	ils voient	ils ont vu	
	elles voient	elles ont vu	

Imparfait Imperfect	Futur Future	Conditionnel Conditional	Passé simple Past Historic
je voyais	je verrai	je verrais	
tu voyais	tu verras	tu verrais	
il/elle/on voyait	il/elle/on verra	il/elle/on verrait	il/elle/on vit
nous voyions	nous verrons	nous verrions	
vous voyiez	vous verrez	vous verriez	
ils/elles voyaient	ils/elles verront	ils/elles verraient	ils/elles virent

vouloir - to want, to wish   for English tense meanings see pages 6 and 7

Impératif Imperative	Présent Present	Passé composé Perfect	
	je veux	j'ai voulu	
veuille!	tu veux	tu as voulu	
	il veut	il a voulu	
	elle veut	elle a voulu	
	on veut	on a voulu	
veuillons!	nous voulons	nous avons voulu	
veuillez!	vous voulez	vous avez voulu	
	ils veulent	ils ont voulu	
	elles veulent	elles ont voulu	

Imparfait Imperfect	Futur Future	Conditionnel Conditional	Passé simple Past Historic
je voulais	je voudrai	je *voudr*ais	
tu voulais	tu voudras	tu *voudr*ais	
il/elle/on voulait	il/elle/on voudra	il/elle/on ---ait	il/elle/on voulut
nous voulions	nous voudrons	nous ---ions	
vous vouliez	vous voudrez	vous ---iez	
ils/elles voulaient	ils/elles voudront	ils/elles ---aient	ils/elles voulurent

SECTION 4 - FRENCH - ENGLISH INDEX

The page references under 'Pg' show the page where the verb is printed, or (for a regular **-er**, **-ir** or **-re** verb) where the pattern verb is printed. All regular **-er** verbs are shown with page 13 as their page reference, but the pattern is printed on page 12. For some verbs there is additional information on the pages given in italics after the English meanings.
See pages 6 and 7 for details of English Tense meanings.

* verb takes **être** in perfect and pluperfect tenses
sthg = something   s.o. = someone

FRENCH	ENGLISH	Pg	FRENCH	ENGLISH	Pg
abandonner	*to abandon*	13	applaudir	*to applaud*	26
abîmer	*to spoil*	13	apporter	*to bring (thing)*	13
aboyer	*to bark*	24	apprendre (à)	*to learn* 10	29
accélérer	*to accelerate*	22	approcher	*to put near*	13
accepter	*to accept*	13	s'approcher de*	*to approach*	16
accompagner	*to accompany*	13	appuyer	*to lean*	24
accrocher	*to hang up*	13	arracher	*to pull out (hair)*	13
accueillir	*to welcome* 26	37	arranger	*to arrange*	18
acheter	*to buy*	21	arrêter	*to arrest* 16	13
achever	*to finish*	21	s'arrêter* (de)	*to stop* 11	16
admirer	*to admire*	13	arriver*	*to arrive* 1, 8, 14	14
adopter	*to adopt*	*13*	s'asseoir*	*to sit down* 4	30
adorer	*to adore* 10	13	assiérai, assiérais	*see s'asseoir**	30
affliger	*to afflict*	*18*	assis	*see s'asseoir**	30
agacer	*to annoy*	17	assister (à)	*to be present at*	13
agiter	*to wave (hand)*	13	s'assit, s'assirent	*sat down*	30
agrandir	*to enlarge*	26	attendre	*to wait (for)* 11	27
aider	*to help*	13	atterrir	*to land (plane)*	26
aie!	*have!*	30	attraper	*to catch*	13
aimer	*to like, to love* 9, 10	13	aurai, aurais	*see avoir*	30
ajouter	*to add*	13	avaler	*to swallow*	13
aller*	*to go* 1, 4, 10	29	avancer	*to advance*	17
allonger	*to lengthen* 16	18	avoir	*to have* 1, 2, 5, 14	30
s'allonger*	*to lie down* 16	18	ayez!	*have!*	30
allumer	*to light, switch on*	13	ayons!	*let's have!*	30
alunir	*to land on the moon*	26	se baigner*	*to bathe*	15
aménager	*to fit out (room)*	18	se balader*	*to go for a walk*	15
amener	*to bring (person)*	21	balayer	*to sweep*	23
amuser	*to amuse*	13	bâtir	*to build*	26
s'amuser*	*to have a good time*	16	battre	*to beat*	31
annoncer	*to announce*	17	bavarder	*to chat*	13
appeler	*to call*	20	blesser	*to wound*	13
s'appeler*	*to be called*	20	se blesser*	*to injure oneself*	15

FRENCH	ENGLISH	Pg	FRENCH	ENGLISH	Pg
boire	*to drink*	31	couler	*to flow, to leak*	13
bouger	*to move*	18	couper	*to cut*	13
bricoler	*to do odd jobs*	13	se couper*	*to cut (finger)*	15
briller	*to shine (sun)*	13	courir	*to run*	35
se bronzer*	*to sunbathe*	15	cousit, cousirent	*sewed*	34
se brosser*	*to brush (hair)*	15	cousu	*see coudre*	34
brûler	*to burn*	13	coûter	*to cost*	13
bu	*see boire*	31	couvrir	*to cover* 26	35
but, burent	*drank*	31	craignit/craignirent	*feared*	36
buvez!	*drink!*	31	craindre	*to be afraid of* 11	36
buvons!	*let's drink!*	31	crier	*to shout*	13
cacher	*to hide (something)*	13	croire	*to believe (in)*	36
se cacher*	*to hide*	15	cru	*see croire*	36
calculer	*to calculate*	13	crut, crurent	*believed*	36
camper	*to camp*	13	cueillir	*to pick* 26	37
casser	*to break*	13	cultiver	*to cultivate*	13
se casser*	*to break (arm)*	15	danser	*to dance*	13
causer	*to chat*	13	se débrouiller*	*to manage, to cope*	15
céder	*to give in*	22	décider (de)	*to decide* 11	13
cesser (de)	*to stop* 11	13	déclarer	*to announce*	13
changer	*to change*	18	découvrir	*to discover* 26	37
chanter	*to sing*	13	déjeuner	*to have lunch*	13
charger	*to load*	18	demander (à)	*to ask* 10, 16	13
chercher	*to look for* 11	13	se demander*	*to wonder* 16	15
choisir	*to choose*	26	déménager	*to move house*	18
coincer	*to block*	17	demeurer	*to live, to remain*	13
collectionner	*to collect*	13	démolir	*to demolish*	26
coller	*to stick (glue)*	13	se dépêcher* (de)	*to hurry* 11	15
commander	*to order (food)*	13	dépenser	*to spend (money)*	13
commencer (à)	*to begin* 10	17	déplacer	*to move (sthg)*	17
communiquer	*to communicate*	13	déranger	*to disturb*	18
compléter	*to complete*	22	descendre*	*to come/go down* 1	28
comprendre	*to understand*	32	se déshabiller*	*to get undressed*	15
compter	*to count, rely on* 10	13	désirer	*to want, to wish* 10	13
conduire	*to drive* 5, 16	32	dessiner	*to draw*	13
se conduire*	*to behave*	16	détester	*to detest* 10	13
connaître	*to know (person)*	33	détruire	*to destroy*	38
conseiller	*to advise*	13	devenir*	*to become* 1	38
considérer	*to consider*	22	deviner	*to guess*	13
construire	*to build*	33	devint, devinrent	*became*	38
contenir	*to contain*	34	devoir	*to have to* 10	39
contint, continrent	*contained*	34	devrai, devrais	*see devoir*	39
continuer (à)	*to continue* 10	13	dîner	*to have dinner*	13
corriger	*to correct*	18	se diriger* (vers)	*to go towards*	18
se coucher*	*to go to bed* 8	15	dire (de)	*to say, to tell* 11	39
se coucher*	*to lie down* 8	15	discuter	*to chat*	13
coudre	*to sew*	34	disparaître	*to disappear*	40

FRENCH	ENGLISH	Pg	FRENCH	ENGLISH	Pg
interroger	*to question*	18	obliger	*to oblige*	18
inventer	*to invent*	13	obtenir	*to obtain*	47
inviter	*to invite*	13	offrir	*to offer* 26	48
irai, irais	*see aller**	29	ont	*see avoir*	30
irriter	*to irritate*	13	opposer	*to oppose*	13
jeter	*to throw*	19	oublier (de)	*to forget* 11	13
jouer (à)/(de)	*to play* 9, 10, 11	13	ouvert	*see ouvrir*	48
juger	*to judge*	18	ouvrir	*to open* 26	48
laisser	*to leave, to allow*	13	paraître	*to appear, to seem*	49
lancer	*to throw*	17	parler	*to speak* 9	13
laver	*to wash*	13	partager	*to share*	18
se laver*	*to get washed* 3	15	partir*	*to leave, go away* 26	49
lever	*to lift* 16	21	paru	*see paraître*	49
se lever*	*to get up* 8, 16	21	parut, parurent	*appeared, seemed*	49
lire	*to read*	44	passer	*to spend time* 10	13
loger	*to live, to lodge*	18	se passer*	*to happen*	15
longer	*to go along*	18	payer	*to pay (for)* 11	23
louer	*to hire, to rent*	13	se peigner*	*to comb one's hair*	15
lu	*see lire*	44	peindre	*to paint*	50
lut, lurent	*read*	44	pendre	*to hang*	27
manger	*to eat* 8	18	penser (à)/(de)	*to think* 8, 10, 11	13
manifester	*to demonstrate*	13	percer	*to pierce*	17
manquer	*to miss*	13	perdre	*to lose*	27
se maquiller*	*to put on make-up*	15	permettre (de)	*to allow* 11	50
marcher	*to walk*	13	permis	*see permettre*	50
mélanger	*to mix*	18	persuader	*to persuade*	13
menacer	*to threaten*	17	peser	*to weigh*	21
mener	*to lead*	21	peux, peut	*see pouvoir*	51
mentir	*lie, tell untruth* 26	45	photocopier	*to photocopy*	13
mettre	*to put*	45	piger *(slang)*	*to understand*	18
se mettre* (à)	*to start (to)* 10	46	pincer	*to pinch*	17
mis	*see mettre*	45	piquer	*to sting, to inject*	13
mit, mirent	*put*	45	placer	*to place*	17
monter*	*to go up, to climb* 1	14	pleurer	*to weep*	13
montrer	*to show*	13	pleut	*see pleuvoir*	51
mort	*see mourir**	46	pleuvoir	*to rain*	51
mourir*	*to die* 1	46	plier	*to fold*	13
mourut, moururent	*died*	46	plonger	*to dive*	18
naître*	*to be born* 1	47	plut	*rained*	51
nager	*to swim* 10	18	polluer	*to pollute*	13
naquit, naquirent	*was/were born*	47	porter	*to carry, to wear*	13
né	*see naître**	47	poser	*to put*	13
négliger	*to neglect*	18	posséder	*to possess*	22
neiger	*to snow*	18	pourrai, pourrais	*see pouvoir*	51
nettoyer	*to clean*	24	pousser	*to push*	13
nommer	*to name*	13	pouvoir	*to be able to* 10	51
noter	*to note*	13	pratiquer	*to practise*	13

SECTION 5 - ENGLISH - FRENCH INDEX

The page references under 'Pg' show where the verb is printed, or (for a regular
-er, -ir or **-re** verb) where the pattern verb is printed. All regular **-er** verbs are
shown with page 13 as their page reference, but the pattern is printed on page 12.
For some verbs there is additional information on the pages given in italics after the
French meanings.
See pages 6 and 7 for details of English Tense meanings.

* verb takes **être** in perfect and pluperfect tenses
sthg = something   s.o. = someone

ENGLISH	FRENCH		Pg
to abandon	*abandonner*		13
to accelerate	*accélérer*		22
to accept	*accepter*		13
to accompany	*accompagner*		13
to add	*ajouter*		13
to admire	*admirer*		13
to adopt	*adopter*		13
to adore	*adorer*	*10*	13
to advance	*avancer*		17
to advise	*conseiller*		13
to afflict	*affliger*		18
to allow	*laisser*		13
to allow	*permettre (de)*	*11*	50
to amuse	*amuser*		13
to announce	*annoncer*		17
to announce	*déclarer*		13
to annoy	*agacer*		17
to annoy	*ennuyer*	*16*	24
to answer	*répondre*	*5*	27
to apologise	*s'excuser**		16
to appear	*paraître*		49
to applaud	*applaudir*		26
to approach	*s'approcher de**		16
to arrange	*arranger*		18
to arrest	*arrêter*	*16*	13
to arrive	*arriver**	*1, 8, 16*	14
to ask	*demander (à)* *10, 16*		13
ate	*see manger*		18
to avenge	*venger*		18
to avoid	*éviter*		13
to bark	*aboyer*		24
to bathe	*se baigner**		15
to be	*être*	*2, 4, 5*	43

ENGLISH	FRENCH		Pg
to be able to	*pouvoir*	*10*	51
to be afraid of	*craindre*	*11*	36
to be alive	*vivre*		63
to be bored	*s'ennuyer**	*16*	24
to be born	*naître**	*1*	47
to be called	*s'appeler**		20
been	*see être*		43
to be interested in	*s'intéresser* (à)* *10*		16
to be present at	*assister (à)*		13
to be situated	*se trouver**	*16*	15
to beat	*battre*		31
to become	*devenir**	*1*	38
to begin	*commencer (à)*	*10*	17
to begin again	*recommencer*		17
to believe (in)	*croire*		36
to block	*coincer*		17
to blow	*souffler*		13
to blush	*rougir*		26
to borrow	*emprunter*		13
bought	*see acheter*		21
to break	*casser*		13
to break (arm)	*se casser**		15
to breathe	*respirer*		13
to bring (person)	*amener*		21
to bring (thing_	*apporter*		13
to bring back	*ramener*		21
to brush (hair)	*se brosser**		15
to build	*bâtir*		26
to build	*construire*		33
to burn	*brûler*		13
to burst	*éclater*		13
to buy	*acheter*		21
to calculate	*calculer*		13

ENGLISH	FRENCH		Pg	ENGLISH	FRENCH		Pg
to finish	*achever*		21	to hang up	*accrocher*		13
to fit out (room)	*aménager*		18	to happen	*se passer**		15
to flow	*couler*		13	to have	*avoir*	2, 5, 14	30
to fly	*voler*		13	to have a good time	*s'amuser**		16
to fold	*plier*		13	to have dinner	*dîner*		13
to follow	*suivre*		61	to have lunch	*déjeuner*		13
to forget	*oublier (de)*	*11*	13	to have to	*devoir*	*10*	39
forgotten	*see oublier (de)*		13	to have to	*falloir (il faut)*	*10*	44
found	*see trouver*		13	to hear	*entendre*		27
to freeze	*geler*		21	held	*see tenir*		62
to frown	*froncer les sourcils*		17	to help	*aider*		13
frozen	*see geler*		21	to help oneself	*se servir**		58
gave	*see donner*		13	to hesitate	*hésiter (à)*	*10*	13
to get angry	*se fâcher**		15	to hide (something)	*cacher*		13
to get divorced	*divorcer*		17	to hide	*se cacher**		15
to get dressed	*s'habiller**		16	to hire	*louer*		13
to get old	*vieillir*		26	to hit	*frapper*		13
to get undressed	*se déshabiller**		15	to hold	*tenir*	*16*	62
to get up	*se lever**	*8, 16*	21	to hold back	*retenir*		55
to get washed	*se laver**	*3*	15	to hope	*espérer*	*10*	22
to give	*donner*	*5*	13	to hurry	*se dépêcher* (de)*	*11*	15
to give back	*rendre*	*16*	27	to imagine	*imaginer*		13
to give in	*céder*		22	to imitate	*imiter*		13
to give up (a habit)	*renoncer (à)*		17	to inform	*informer*		13
to gnaw	*ronger*		18	to inform	*prévenir*		52
to go	*aller**	*1, 4, 10*	29	to inject	*piquer*		13
to go along	*longer*		18	to injure oneself	*se blesser**		15
to go around with	*fréquenter*		13	to invent	*inventer*		13
to go away	*partir**	*1, 26*	49	to invite	*inviter*		13
to go for a walk	*se balader*		15	to iron	*repasser*		13
to go for a walk	*se promener**	*16*	21	to irritate	*irriter*		13
gone	*see aller**		29	to judge	*juger*		18
to go out	*sortir**	*1, 26*	59	to jump	*sauter*		13
to go red	*rougir*		26	to keep	*garder*		13
to go to bed	*se coucher**	*8*	15	to keep	*tenir*		62
to go to sleep	*s'endormir**		41	to keep (hold back)	*retenir*		55
to go towards	*se diriger* vers*		18	to kill	*tuer*		13
to go up	*monter**	*1*	14	knew	*see connaître*		33
to greet	*saluer*		13	knew	*see savoir*		56
grew	*see grandir*		26	to knock	*frapper*		13
to grow	*grandir*		26	to know (place)	*connaître*		33
to grumble	*grogner*	*11*	13	to know (fact)	*savoir*	*10*	56
to grumble	*râler (slang)*		13	to land on moon	*alunir*		26
to guess	*deviner*		13	to land (plane)	*atterrir*		26
to guide	*guider*		13	to last	*durer*		13
had	*see avoir*		30	to laugh	*rire*		56
to hang	*pendre*		27	to laugh	*rigoler*		13

ENGLISH	FRENCH		Pg
ran	*see courir*		35
rang	*see sonner*		13
to read	*lire*		44
to receive	*recevoir*		53
to recognise	*reconnaître*		53
to record	*enregistrer*		13
to recycle	*recycler*		13
to redouble (effort)	*redoubler*		13
to refuse (to)	*refuser (de)*	*11*	13
to regret	*regretter (de)*	*11*	13
to relieve	*soulager*		18
to rely on	*compter sur*	*10*	13
to remain	*demeurer*		13
to remember	*se rappeler**	*16*	20
to remember	*se souvenir*(de)*	*11*	60
to remind	*rappeler*	*16*	20
to remove	*enlever*		21
to rent	*louer*		13
to repair	*réparer*		13
to repeat	*répéter*		22
to replace	*remplacer*		17
to reply	*répondre*	*5*	27
to reply	*répliquer*		13
to reserve	*réserver*		13
to rest	*se reposer**		15
to resume	*reprendre*		54
to return	*revenir**	*1*	51
to reveal	*révéler*		22
to ring	*sonner*		13
to risk	*risquer*		13
to run	*courir*		35
to run away	*se sauver**		15
to sack	*renvoyer*		25
said	*see dire*		39
sat down	*see s'asseoir**		30
saw (to see)	*see voir*		64
to say	*dire*	*11*	39
to scold	*gronder*		13
to see	*voir*	*4*	64
to seem	*paraître*		49
to seem	*sembler*		13
seen	*see voir*		64
to seize	*saisir*		26
to sell	*vendre*		27
to send	*envoyer*		25
sent	*see envoyer*		25
to separate	*séparer*		13

ENGLISH	FRENCH		Pg
to serve	*servir*	*26*	58
to settle	*régler*		22
to sew	*coudre*		34
to share	*partager*		18
to shave	*se raser**		15
to shine (sun)	*briller*		13
to shout	*crier*		13
to show	*montrer*		13
to sigh	*soupirer*		13
to sing	*chanter*		13
to sit down	*s'asseoir**	*4*	30
to sleep	*dormir*		40
slept	*see dormir*		40
to slip	*glisser*		13
to smell	*sentir*	*11, 16, 26*	57
to smile	*sourire*		60
to smoke	*fumer*		13
to snow	*neiger*		18
sold	*see acheter*		21
to sort out	*régler*		22
to speak	*parler*	*9*	13
to spend (money)	*dépenser*		13
to spend (time)	*passer*	*10*	13
to spoil	*abîmer*		13
spoke	*see parler*		13
spoken	*see parler*		13
to squash	*écraser*		13
to squeeze	*serrer*		13
to stand	*se tenir**	*16*	62
to start to	*se mettre* (à)*	*10*	46
to stay	*rester**	*1*	14
to stick (glue)	*coller*		13
to sting	*piquer*		13
stood	*see se tenir**		62
to stop	*s'arrêter* (de)*	*11*	16
to stop	*cesser (de)*	*11*	13
to strengthen	*renforcer*		17
to study	*étudier*		13
to succeed (in)	*réussir (à)*	*10*	26
to suck	*sucer*		17
to suffer	*souffrir*	*26*	59
to suggest	*proposer*		13
to suggest	*suggérer*		22
to sunbathe	*se bronzer**		15
to suppose	*supposer*		13
to surprise	*surprendre*		61
to surrender	*se rendre**	*16*	28

ENGLISH	FRENCH		Pg		ENGLISH	FRENCH		Pg
to suspect	*soupçonner*		13		understood	*see comprendre*		32
to swallow	*avaler*		13		to use	*employer*		24
to sweep	*balayer*		23		to use	*se servir *(de)*	26	58
to swim	*nager*	10	18		to use	*utiliser*		13
to switch on	*allumer*		13		to visit (place)	*visiter*	8	13
to take	*prendre*	5	52		to vote	*voter*		13
to take away	*emporter*		13		to wait (for)	*attendre*	8	27
to take back	*reprendre*		54		to wake someone	*réveiller*		13
to take care of	*soigner*		13		to wake up	*se réveiller**		15
to take for a walk	*promener*	16	21		to walk	*marcher*		13
to take the place of	*remplacer*		17		to walk about	*se balader**		15
to take with you	*emmener*		21		to want	*désirer*	10	13
to taste	*goûter*		13		to want	*vouloir*	10	64
to teach	*enseigner*		13		to warn	*prévenir*		52
to tell	*dire (de)*	11	39		was	*see être*		43
to tell (story)	*raconter*		13		to wash	*laver*		13
to tell untruth	*mentir*	26	45		to wash oneself	*se laver**	3	15
to thank	*remercier*		13		to wave (hand)	*agiter*		13
to think	*penser (à)*	8, 10	13		to wear	*porter*		13
to think	*penser (de)*	8, 11	13		to weep	*pleurer*		13
to think (reflect)	*réfléchir*		26		to weigh	*peser*		21
thought	*see penser*		13		to welcome	*accueillir*	26	37
to threaten	*menacer*		17		wept	*see pleurer*		13
threw	*see jeter*		19		were	*see être*		43
to throw	*jeter*		19		to win	*gagner*		13
to throw	*lancer*		17		to wipe	*essuyer*		24
to tidy	*ranger*		18		to wish	*désirer*	10	13
to tire out	*fatiguer*		13		to wish	*vouloir*	10	64
told	*see dire*		39		to witness	*témoigner*		13
took	*see prendre*		52		to wonder	*se demander**	16	15
to touch	*toucher*		13		to work	*travailler*	6, 7	12
to travel	*voyager*		18		to worry	*s'inquiéter**		22
to travel (vehicle)	*rouler*		13		to worry someone	*troubler*		13
to tremble	*trembler*		13		to worry someone	*inquiéter*		22
tried	*see essayer (de)*		23		to wound	*blesser*		13
to try (food)	*goûter*		13		to write	*écrire*	11	41
to try (to)	*essayer (de)*	11	23		to write (essay)	*rédiger*		18
to turn	*tourner*		13		written	*see écrire*		41
to understand	*comprendre*		32		wrote	*see écrire*		41
to understand	*piger (slang)*		18					

SECTION 6 - GRAMMAR INDEX

TO FIND A VERB IN THIS BOOK

- Check the index: French-English   see pages 65-70

                             English-French   see pages 71-76

- If the verb is not listed, in the index, follow these guidelines, which may help:

	If the infinitive ends in –**ir**	see page 26
	If the infinitive ends in –**re**	see page 27-28
	If the infinitive ends in –**er**	see page 12-16
But:	If the infinitive ends in –**cer**	see page 17
	If the infinitive ends in –**ger**	see page 18
	If the infinitive ends in –**eler**	see page 20
	If the infinitive ends in –**e-consonant-er**	see page 21
	If the infinitive ends in –**é-consonant-er**	see page 22
	If the infinitive ends in –**ayer**	see page 23
	If the infinitive ends in –**oyer**	see page 24-25
	If the infinitive ends in –**uyer**	see page 24-25

- Check the basic form of the infinitive. The verb may have a prefix such as:

d-	dé**crire**	see page 41		pro-	pro**mettre**	see page 45
dé-	dé**battre**	see page 31		pour-	pour**suivre**	see page 61
dis-	dis**poser**	see page 13		re-	re**partir***	see page 49
entre-	entre**prendre**	see page 52		ré-	ré**ouvrir**	see page 48
par-	par**courir**	see page 35		ren-	se ren**dormir**	see page 40
per-	per**mettre**	see page 45		sur-	sur**vivre**	see page 63
pré-	pré**dire**	see page 39		trans-	trans**mettre**	see page 45

  and be a compound of a verb which is listed.

- If the verb is a newly invented or imported verb it will follow the regular **-er** pattern:

  programmer, radioguider, synthéthiser, zigzaguer   see page 12

- Reflexive verbs are listed in the indexes under the first letter of the infinitive:

  se **promener**   see page 21

  Some verbs may be used both reflexively and non-reflexively (see page 16), but there is one important difference. When they are used reflexively they take **être** in the perfect tense:

          je me suis levé(e)   *I got up*

  See page 5 for the pattern showing the agreements of the past participle.

  When they are used non-reflexively they usually take **avoir** in the perfect tense

          j'ai levé   *I lifted*

- To make a verb negative   see page 8

- To make a verb into a question   see page 9

- To check the English meanings of a tense   see pages 6-7